Mind your own GCSE business with CGP!

Doing well in business is all about hard work, determination and giving your customers what they want. The same goes for GCSE Business, except you have to give the examiners what they want. And they're the pickiest customers of all...

Not to worry. This brilliant CGP Revision Guide covers everything you'll need to know for the Grade 9-1 AQA course, from enterprise to e-commerce.

We've also included plenty of practice questions and top advice to help you score market-leading results in the exams!

CGP — still the best! ☺

Our sole aim here at CGP is to produce the highest quality books — carefully written, immaculately presented and dangerously close to being funny.

Then we work our socks off to get them out to you — at the cheapest possible prices.

Contents

Section 1 — Business in the Real World

Why Businesses Exist...2

Enterprise...3

Factors of Production...4

Business Ownership Structures.............................5

More Business Ownership Structures...................6

Choosing a Business Ownership Structure..........7

Business Aims and Objectives.................................8

More on Business Objectives..................................9

Stakeholders..10

Revenue, Costs and Profit......................................11

The Business Plan...12

Location..13

Expanding Businesses...14

Internal Expansion...15

External Expansion..16

Case Study — Business in the Real World.........17

Revision Summary..18

Section 2 — Influences on Business

Employment and the Law..19

Consumer Law...20

Technology and Business..21

Ethical Considerations..22

Environmental Influences......................................23

Unemployment and Consumer Spending..........24

Interest Rates..25

Competition...26

Globalisation...27

Exchange Rates...28

Risks in Business..29

Case Study — Influences on Business................30

Revision Summary..31

Section 3 — Business Operations

Supply Chains..32

More on Supply Chains...33

Methods of Production...34

Production Efficiency..35

Quality..36

Quality Management..37

Customer Service..38

More on Customer Service.....................................39

Case Study — Business Operations......................40

Revision Summary..41

Section 4 — Human Resources

Internal Organisational Structures......................42

More on Internal Organisational Structures......43

Other Internal Organisational Structures...........44

Contracts of Employment.......................................45

Recruitment...46

More on Recruitment...47

Staff Training...48

Financial Motivation..49

Non-Financial Motivation......................................50

Case Study — Human Resources..........................51

Revision Summary..52

Section 5 — Marketing

The Marketing Mix...53

Market Research...54

Types of Market Research......................................55

Using Market Research..56

Product Life Cycles..57

Extension Strategies..58

Product Portfolios..59

Product Development...60

More on Product Development..............................61

Price...62

Pricing Strategies..63

Methods of Promotion.......................................64

More Methods of Promotion.............................65

Place..66

E-Commerce...67

More on E-Commerce...68

Case Study — Marketing....................................69

Revision Summary...70

Income Statements...79

Analysis — Income Statements..........................80

Profit Margins...81

Statements of Financial Position........................82

More on Statements of Financial Position..........83

Analysis — Statements of Financial Position......84

Analysis — Competitors......................................85

Case Study — Finance..86

Revision Summary...87

Section 6 — Finance

Sources of Finance — Small Firms......................71

Sources of Finance — Established Firms.............72

Investments..73

Break-Even Analysis..74

More on Break-Even Analysis.............................75

Cash Flow...76

Cash Flow — Credit..77

Cash Flow — Problems.......................................78

What to Expect in the Exams

The Exams...88

Answering Questions..89

Answers...90

Glossary..92

Index...97

Published by CGP

Based on the classic CGP style created by Richard Parsons

Editors: Charlotte Burrows, Emily Howe, Ciara McGlade and Rachael Rogers

Contributor: Colin Harber-Stuart

ISBN: 978 1 78294 689 2

With thanks to Glenn Rogers and Victoria Skelton for the proofreading.

With thanks to Ana Pungartnik for the copyright research.

Pages 8, 24 and 30 contain information from the Office for National Statistics licensed under the Open Government Licence v3.0.
http://www.nationalarchives.gov.uk/doc/open-government-licence/version/3/

Printed by Elanders Ltd, Newcastle upon Tyne.
Clipart from Corel®

Why Businesses Exist

Businesses don't <u>only</u> exist so that you can take a GCSE in Business... They provide lots of other <u>useful</u> things as well. Like chocolate, stationery, or the purple velvet hat I bought last week.

Businesses Supply Goods or Services

1) Businesses <u>sell products</u> to <u>customers</u> who are willing to pay for them.

2) Products can be <u>goods</u> or <u>services</u>:
   - <u>Goods</u> are <u>physical items</u> like books or furniture.
   - <u>Services</u> are <u>actions</u> performed by other people to aid the customer, e.g. barbers and plumbers provide services.

3) Some businesses provide goods or services that are <u>needs</u> — things that you <u>can't</u> <u>live without</u> (like <u>water</u> and <u>food</u>).

4) Others provide goods or services that are <u>wants</u> — things you would <u>like</u> to have, but can <u>survive without</u> (like holidays and jewellery).

Businesses are Set Up for Various Reasons

Homework Services
You get it, I do it!

Businesses can be set up for a whole <u>host</u> of reasons. Here are the main ones:

1) Some businesses are set up when someone starts making <u>a good</u> or providing <u>a service</u> that they think customers will want to pay for.

2) Some people start businesses that <u>distribute goods</u>. E.g. they <u>buy</u> products from a manufacturer and then <u>sell</u> them on to other businesses or to <u>individual customers</u>.

3) Some businesses are specifically set up to <u>benefit</u> other people. They could make <u>goods</u> or provide a <u>service</u>. For example, there are businesses that organise volunteers to go into <u>schools</u> and help children learn how to <u>read</u>. Many of these businesses are <u>not-for-profit</u> organisations (see p.7).

4) Some people will start a business because they see a <u>business opportunity</u> that they want to fulfil. This is an <u>investment</u> in e.g. equipment, which will allow an individual (or a group of people) to <u>start</u> a business. For example, a person may buy rights to a <u>franchise</u>. This is where they start their own business under the name of <u>another company</u> (see p.15). They may do this if they notice that branches of the company <u>aren't available</u> in their local area.

The Sector a Business is in Tells You What it Provides

There are <u>three sectors</u> of the economy — you need to know what they are.

1) The <u>PRIMARY SECTOR</u> produces <u>raw materials</u> — any <u>natural resources</u> which are used to make goods or services.

2) They can be <u>extracted</u> from the ground. The <u>mining</u> industry provides coal, oil, gas, and metals like iron. The <u>quarrying</u> industry provides stone.

3) They can be <u>grown</u>. E.g. the <u>farming</u> industry grows food (both animals and crops are natural resources).

4) They can be <u>collected</u>. The <u>fishing</u> industry "collects" fish from the sea.

1) The <u>SECONDARY SECTOR</u> manufactures <u>goods</u>. They turn raw materials into finished goods. For example, a <u>chocolate factory</u> turns raw materials such as <u>cocoa</u> and <u>milk</u> into chocolate.

2) The <u>building</u> and <u>construction</u> industries are also in the secondary sector.

1) The <u>TERTIARY SECTOR</u> provides <u>services</u>.

2) Some firms provide services for other <u>businesses</u> — like warehousing and advertising.

3) Some firms provide services for <u>consumers</u> — like hairdressers, shops and restaurants.

4) <u>Financial</u> services like banking and insurance are used by <u>both</u> businesses and consumers.

Let's get down to business...

Well that's an easy enough page to start with. Make sure you know why businesses exist and the reasons why people might start them up. It's not always about getting rich. Sometimes it's just to make the world a better place.

Enterprise

Enterprise can mean <u>either</u> a business or organisation, <u>or</u> the personal qualities that mean you can see and take advantage of new business opportunities (e.g. "That boy will go far — he's got enterprise").

Entrepreneurs Take Advantage of Business Opportunities

1) Enterprise involves <u>identifying</u> new business opportunities, and then <u>taking advantage</u> of them. There's always a <u>risk</u> of <u>failure</u>, but the <u>reward</u> for a successful enterprise activity is usually <u>profit</u>.

2) Enterprise can involve starting up a <u>new business</u>, or helping an existing one to <u>expand</u> by coming up with <u>new ideas</u>.

3) An <u>entrepreneur</u> is someone who takes on the <u>risks</u> of enterprise activity.

Entrepreneurs Have Different Objectives

There are lots of possible <u>reasons</u> why someone might decide to become an <u>entrepreneur</u>. For example...

1) There might be <u>financial reasons</u> — if the business is <u>successful</u> and makes a <u>profit</u>, the entrepreneur could earn more <u>money</u> than they did before. This could give them a better <u>quality of life</u>.

2) Some people start a business when they identify a <u>gap in the market</u> — i.e. they think of a useful <u>good</u> or <u>service</u> that <u>no other</u> business is providing.

> In the 1970s, James Dyson came up with the idea of a <u>vacuum cleaner</u> that didn't need <u>dust bags</u>. <u>Customers</u> wanted to buy the vacuum cleaner, as it meant they no longer had to <u>buy</u> replacement bags and the new vacuum cleaner didn't lose <u>suction</u>.

3) Some people might want the <u>independence</u> of being their own <u>boss</u>. This means they can <u>decide</u> what they <u>do</u> each day, and make the decisions about <u>how</u> the business will be run. They might also enjoy more <u>flexible working hours</u>, meaning it's easier to fit <u>work</u> around <u>other commitments</u>, like <u>childcare</u>.

4) Some people want to follow an <u>interest</u>. E.g. a <u>history-lover</u> might set up a <u>tour company</u> for a historical site. Being <u>interested</u> in what they do can a give a person a lot of <u>job satisfaction</u>.

5) Some people are simply <u>dissatisfied</u> with their <u>current job</u>. Starting up a new business can help them to feel <u>happier</u> and <u>more motivated</u> to go to work.

Entrepreneurs Need Particular Qualities

A <u>successful</u> entrepreneur is likely to have <u>most</u> of the following characteristics:

• <u>Hardworking</u> — it takes a lot of <u>hard work</u> to turn ideas into <u>practice</u>. Entrepreneurs often work <u>long hours</u>. To begin with, they may be working <u>alone</u>, so they have to do all the <u>different tasks</u> involved in running a business, such as <u>accounting</u>, <u>business planning</u> and <u>sales and marketing</u>.

• <u>Organised</u> — entrepreneurs have to have good organisational skills to keep on top of all the <u>day-to-day tasks</u> of running the business as well as <u>planning for the future</u>. E.g. they have to make sure they're properly <u>prepared</u> for meetings and that they're <u>in control</u> of their <u>finances</u>.

• <u>Innovative</u> — to come up with <u>new ideas</u> and think of <u>solutions</u> to <u>problems</u> that come up.

• A <u>willingness</u> to take a calculated <u>risk</u> — there are lots of <u>unknowns</u> involved in running a business. The entrepreneur will probably give up their <u>current job</u> and invest <u>money</u> that they could <u>lose</u> if the business <u>fails</u>. They can write a <u>business plan</u> to work out if the business is a <u>good idea</u> (see p.12), but they can't know exactly what's going to happen before they start.

Enterprise — think Dragons' Den... (or *Star Trek*™ if that's more your thing)

Bit of a funny page this one, all about new ideas and personal qualities and risk-taking. But funny or not, you need to make sure you know everything on this page. Yep, all of it. Even that bit right up there at the top.

Factors of Production

Things wouldn't work if there weren't any resources. For example, I need food, sleep and lots of tea...

There are Four Factors of Production

Resources are needed to make products. Resources can be divided into four factors of production.
These factors are: land, labour, capital and enterprise.

1 — Land

As well as actual 'territory', land includes all the Earth's natural resources:
1) Non-renewable resources, such as natural gas, oil and coal.
2) Renewable resources like wind or tidal power, or wood from trees.
3) Materials extracted by mining (e.g. diamonds and gold).
4) Water.
5) Animals found in an area.

Nearly all things that fall under the category of 'land' are scarce —
there aren't enough natural resources to satisfy the demands of everyone.

Individuals and firms are rewarded for providing these factors, e.g. with wages, rent, interest or profit.

2 — Labour

1) Labour is the work done by the people who contribute to the production process.
2) Different people have different levels of education, experience or training. These factors can make some people more 'valuable' or productive in the workplace than others.

3 — Capital

1) Capital is the equipment, factories and schools that help to produce goods or services.
2) Capital is different from land because capital has to be made first.

4 — Enterprise

Enterprise refers to the people (entrepreneurs) who take risks and create things from the other three factors of production (see previous page).

Opportunity Costs Help People Choose How to Use Resources

1) Most factors of production are limited. To work out the best way to use them, managers will often look at the opportunity cost of a decision.

2) Opportunity cost is the benefit that's given up in order to do something else — it's the cost of the choice that's made. It's the idea that money or time spent doing one thing is likely to mean missing out on doing something else.

3) So it puts a value on the product or business decision in terms of what the business had to give up to make it.

4) Businesses must choose where to use their limited resources. Managers compare opportunity costs when making decisions.

Opportunity cost of revision: fun.

BUSINESS EXAMPLE

- Go-Kart Village have £10 000 to invest in their business.
- They could spend the money on some new go-karts or on redecorating their building.
- If they choose to redecorate, the opportunity cost is the new go-karts and the extra money they could have made from people using them.

5) In more formal terms, opportunity cost is the value of the next best alternative that's been given up.

I bought a rabbit for £25 — I thought about the hopportunity cost first...

Managers need to know what resources they have and then they need to find the best way to use those resources.

Business Ownership Structures

Every business needs to have an appropriate legal structure. There are a few types you need to know about, covered here and on the next page. You should know what they are, the differences between them and the advantages and disadvantages of each.

Sole Traders — the Easiest Business to Start

Sole trader businesses have just one owner (though the owner may employ other people to work for them). Most small businesses are sole traders. You don't need to do much except start trading. Examples include plumbers, hairdressers, newsagents and fishmongers.

 I'm a sole trader

Sole traders — advantages

1) They're easy to set up, which means they're great for start-up businesses.
2) You get to be your own boss.
3) You alone decide what happens to any profit.

Sole traders — disadvantages

1) You might have to work long hours and may not get many holidays.
2) You have unlimited liability. This means that if the business goes bust owing £10 million, you are liable (legally responsible) for paying back all of the debt — which might mean you have to sell everything you own.
3) You're unincorporated. This means the business doesn't have its own legal identity. So if anyone sues the business, they'll sue you personally.
4) It can be hard to raise money. Banks see sole traders as risky, so it may be hard to get a loan. You often have to rely on your own savings, or family and friends.

Some companies have limited liability — which means the amount of debt the owners have to pay back is limited to the amount they invested (see next page).

For more about finding finance for a business, see p.71-72.

Partnerships are Like Two or More Sole Traders

You get partnerships in businesses like accountancy firms, solicitors and doctors' surgeries. Partnerships generally have between two and twenty partners. Each partner has an equal say in making decisions and an equal share of the profits — unless they have an agreement called a deed of partnership that says different.

Partnerships — advantages

1) More owners means more ideas, and a greater range of skills and expertise — e.g. one partner might be great at sales, while another is good at planning.
2) It also means more people to share the work.
3) More owners means more capital (money) can be put into the business, so it can grow faster.

Partnerships — disadvantages

1) Each partner is legally responsible for what all the other partners do.
2) Like sole traders, most partnerships have unlimited liability (see above).
3) More owners means more disagreements. You're not the only boss. If the partners disagree about which direction the business should go in and how much time to put in, it can get unpleasant.
4) The profits are shared between the partners. So if a sole trader decides to go into partnership with another person, they could end up with less money for themselves.

About turn! *Full steam ahead!* Partner

PRACTICE QUESTION ## *Wanted: Soul Trader — must have own hood and scythe...*

Q1 Jennifer is a sole trader who owns a shoe shop. She is thinking about going into partnership with her brother. Explain one advantage and one disadvantage of Jennifer going into the partnership.

More Business Ownership Structures

The final two types of business are <u>more expensive</u> to set up than the ones on the previous page. But they carry <u>less financial risk</u> for the owners.

Limited Companies Are Owned by Shareholders

Hmm... there's limited company in this bar

There are <u>two types</u> of limited company — <u>private</u> and <u>public</u>. But <u>both kinds</u> have some important differences compared to sole traders and partnerships:

1) A limited company is <u>incorporated</u> — it has a <u>separate legal identity</u> from the owners. So any money, property, tax bills, etc. in the company's name <u>belong to the company</u>, not the owners.

2) Being incorporated means the owners have <u>limited liability</u>. If anything goes wrong (e.g. somebody sues the company or it goes bust) it's the <u>company</u> that's <u>liable</u>, <u>not the owners</u>. The owners only <u>risk losing</u> the money that they have <u>invested</u>.

3) It is owned by <u>shareholders</u>. The <u>more shares</u> you own, the <u>more control</u> you get.

Private Limited Companies — Ownership Is Restricted

'<u>Private</u>' means that <u>shares</u> can only be sold if <u>all the shareholders</u> agree. The shareholders are often all members of the same family. Private limited companies have <u>Ltd.</u> after their name.

Ltd. — advantages

1) The <u>big advantage</u> over sole traders and partnerships is <u>limited liability</u> — you can't lose more than you invest.

2) Being <u>incorporated</u>, the company can continue trading after a shareholder <u>dies</u> — unlike partnerships.

3) It's easier for a Ltd. company to get a <u>loan</u> or <u>mortgage</u> than it is for a sole trader or partnership.

4) For someone to buy shares, all the other shareholders have to <u>agree</u>. So the owners keep a lot of <u>control</u> over how the business is managed and how many people get to <u>share</u> the <u>profits</u>.

Ltd. — disadvantages

1) They're <u>more expensive</u> to set up than partnerships because of all the <u>legal paperwork</u> you have to do.

2) Unlike sole traders or partnerships, the company is <u>legally obliged</u> to <u>publish its accounts</u> every year (although they <u>don't</u> have to be made <u>public</u>).

It's hard for someone to take over a Ltd. company — to do so, all the shareholders of the Ltd. company would have to agree to sell shares.

Public Limited Companies — Anyone Can Buy Shares

'<u>Public</u>' means that the company <u>shares</u> are traded on a <u>stock exchange</u>, and can be bought and sold by <u>anyone</u>. Firms often become public limited companies when they want to <u>expand</u>. Public limited companies have '<u>PLC</u>' after their name.

PLC — advantages

1) Much more <u>capital</u> can be raised by a PLC than by any other kind of business.

2) That helps the company to <u>expand</u> and <u>diversify</u>.

3) Like private limited companies, they also have the benefits of having <u>limited liability</u>, and being <u>incorporated</u>.

PLC — disadvantages

1) It can be hard to get lots of shareholders to <u>agree</u> on how the business is <u>run</u>. Each shareholder has <u>very little say</u> (unless they own a <u>lot</u> of shares).

2) It's easy for someone to buy enough shares to <u>take over</u> the company — if they can convince shareholders to sell.

3) The <u>accounts</u> have to be made <u>public</u> — so everyone (including <u>competitors</u>) can see if a business is struggling.

4) More shareholders means there's more people wanting a <u>share of the profits</u>.

Limited lie-ability — you can't help telling the truth...

Most of the shops you see on the high street will be private limited companies or public limited companies. Even CGP is in on the act — have a hunt at the front of the book to see if you can find a little 'Ltd.' after our name.

Choosing a Business Ownership Structure

Choosing the right structure for a business is <u>essential</u> (although you can usually change your mind later).

A Business has to Choose its Legal Structure

1) When you start a new business, you need to decide whether to have <u>limited</u> or <u>unlimited</u> liability.

2) <u>Smaller</u> businesses (sole traders and partnerships) tend to have <u>unlimited liability</u>, while <u>larger</u> businesses have <u>limited liability</u> (they'll be "Ltds" or "PLCs").

3) The other thing to decide is the amount of <u>control</u> you want over how the business is run. <u>Sole traders</u> and <u>private limited companies</u> (Ltds) tend to give an entrepreneur <u>more</u> control than partnerships or PLCs.

4) Businesses don't have to keep the structure they start off with — the structure can <u>change over time</u>.

5) For example, a <u>sole trader</u> might form a <u>partnership</u> if someone they know (e.g. an employee or family member) wants to <u>invest money</u> into the business in return for a <u>share of the profits</u>.

6) Often, as a business grows, a sole trader or partnership will decide to <u>incorporate</u> the business and may also decide to make shares <u>public</u>. Most <u>very large</u> businesses are <u>public limited companies</u>.

> 1) The supermarket chain <u>Morrisons</u> started when the <u>sole trader</u> William Morrison started trading from a <u>market stall</u> in Bradford. The business did well, and he started to open stores in the Bradford area.
>
> 2) In 1940, the company was <u>incorporated</u> — this would have protected William Morrison's investments, and would have made it easier to raise money so the company could <u>grow more</u>.
>
> 3) The company continued to expand. In <u>1967</u>, the company became a <u>public limited company</u> to help raise the funds so it could <u>expand further</u>.

BUSINESS EXAMPLE

Not-for-Profit Businesses Must Choose a Legal Structure

1) '<u>Not-for-profit</u>' businesses <u>don't</u> try to make a profit (at least, not for their owners).

2) They need to generate enough income to <u>cover their costs</u>, but any <u>surplus</u> is put back into the business or used to <u>fund</u> projects that help the community.

3) There are lots of not-for-profit organisations, and their size and aims can be very different. E.g. a local <u>amateur dramatics</u> society might have 50 members and aim to put on a <u>yearly show</u>, while a <u>larger</u> not-for-profit firm might work in <u>ten different countries</u> and aim to banish <u>world poverty</u>.

4) Many not-for-profit organisations have <u>charitable status</u>. This means they get some <u>tax relief</u> and they're able to apply for certain <u>grants</u>. But they can be hard to set up as there are lots of <u>rules</u> they have to follow. Also, many charities are funded mainly by <u>donations</u> and <u>grants</u> — which means they may <u>not</u> have a <u>stable income</u>.

Charities and social enterprises are types of organisation — they are not legal structures.

5) <u>Social enterprises</u> are another type of not-for-profit organisation. These make money by <u>selling products</u> — they are similar to 'for-profit' businesses but their aims are always centred around using their profits to <u>benefit society</u> in some way. As they <u>make their own profit</u> through what they sell, they <u>don't</u> rely as heavily on donations and grants as many charities.

6) Not-for-profit firms can be <u>hard to manage</u>, particularly if there's always <u>uncertainty</u> about how much <u>finance</u> they'll have available, and if they rely on <u>volunteers</u> rather than permanent members of staff.

7) As not-for-profit organisations can be so varied, there are many <u>different legal structures</u> they can have.

- They can choose to be an '<u>unincorporated association</u>'. These are easy to <u>set up</u> but the people who manage the organisation have <u>unlimited liability</u>.

- Bigger organisations tend to be <u>incorporated</u> so that the people who run them have <u>limited liability</u>. They are often '<u>limited by guarantee</u>', meaning that some of its members guarantee that they'll pay a fixed amount of money on behalf of the business if it <u>goes bust</u>.

My knowledge of business ownership structures is limited...

The business world isn't all about people getting rich — some firms are set up just to make the world a better place.

Business Aims and Objectives

Businesses need to have <u>aims</u> — overall <u>goals</u> that they want to achieve.

Businesses can Have a Variety of Different Aims

Survival

Around <u>60%</u> of new businesses close within five years of starting, so just <u>surviving</u> is the main and most important <u>short-term</u> aim of all new businesses.

Maximise Profit

The vast majority of businesses will aim to <u>maximise profits</u>. However, it may take a few years for a new firm to make any profit at all.

Growth

Many firms will aim to <u>grow</u>, but growth can mean different things. E.g. it might mean <u>increasing the number of employees</u>, <u>increasing the number of products sold</u>, or <u>increasing income from sales</u>.

Some firms want to grow <u>domestically</u> (in the country where they were set up). Others want to grow <u>internationally</u> (expand into <u>other countries</u>).

Increase Shareholder Value

<u>Limited</u> companies have <u>shareholders</u>. Shareholders get a <u>share</u> of the firm's <u>profits</u> and can <u>sell</u> their shares to <u>make money</u> (the better the firm is doing, the more each share is worth). Many firms aim to <u>increase shareholder value</u> (make their shareholders more <u>wealthy</u>) by increasing the <u>value</u> of the firm, e.g. by making <u>more profit</u> or by <u>growing</u>.

Increase Market Share

Market share tells you what <u>percentage</u> of a market's <u>total sales</u> a particular product or company has made. When a business first starts up it has zero market share... so one of its first aims is to capture a part of the market and <u>establish</u> itself. It can then aim to increase its market share by taking sales <u>away</u> from competition, or by persuading <u>new customers</u> to enter the market and buy its products.

Sweet 'n' Sour Chinese has a big market share already, but New Noodles might want to try and increase its share of the market.

Do What's Right Socially and Ethically

Some firms want to make sure they are acting in ways that are <u>best for society</u> and that society believes are <u>morally right</u> (e.g. many consumers think that it's <u>wrong</u> to test cosmetics on animals). They may also want to make sure their activities don't cause unnecessary harm to the <u>environment</u>.

Achieve Customer Satisfaction

<u>Customer satisfaction</u> measures how <u>happy</u> consumers are with the products provided by the firm. The firm can <u>measure</u> this by carrying out <u>customer opinion surveys</u>, a type of <u>market research</u> (see p.55).

Objectives Help Businesses Achieve Their Aims

1) Once a firm has established its aims, it needs to set business <u>objectives</u>.

2) Just like with aims, there are different <u>types</u> of objectives. They can be related to survival, profit, growth, shareholder value, market share, social and ethical issues or customer satisfaction.

3) Objectives are more <u>specific</u> than aims — they're <u>measurable</u> steps on the way to the aim. E.g. if a firm's aim is to <u>grow</u>, an objective might be to increase income from sales by <u>30%</u> over <u>two years</u>.

4) Once objectives have been set they act as <u>clear targets</u> for firms to work towards.

5) They can then be used later to <u>measure</u> whether a firm has been <u>successful</u> or not (next page).

Survival — also the main aim during exam time...

Your aim is to learn this page. Your objectives are to make coffee, read the page through twice and then write down what you remember. Once you understand everything, it's time to find out how to measure success...

More on Business Objectives

More on <u>objectives</u> now — how and why they <u>change</u> and how they're used to <u>measure success</u>. Enjoy.

Not All Companies Have the Same Objectives

There are <u>different factors</u> that affect the objectives of a business:

1) The <u>size</u> of the business — many <u>small</u>, local businesses depend on <u>word of mouth</u> to survive, so a major objective for them might be <u>customer satisfaction</u>. They may be more concerned with <u>survival</u> and <u>growth</u> rather than increasing market share. Larger businesses get more <u>attention</u> from the public, so they might set objectives about <u>acting ethically</u> and protecting the <u>environment</u> to try to avoid bad publicity.

2) The <u>level of competition</u> the business faces — if a business is in a <u>highly competitive</u> market, it might focus on <u>customer satisfaction</u> so that it can <u>win customers</u> from its rivals. Increasing or holding on to its <u>market share</u> might be more important than maximising profits. If a firm doesn't face much competition, its objectives may be focused more on <u>growth</u> and <u>maximising profits</u>.

3) The <u>type</u> of business — e.g. <u>not-for-profit</u> businesses (see p.7) are more likely to focus on <u>social</u> or <u>ethical</u> objectives, rather than growth or profit.

A Company's Objectives can Change over Time

1) A firm will <u>alter</u> its objectives as it <u>evolves</u> (changes). For example, when it is a <u>new</u>, <u>start-up</u> business, objectives will be focused on <u>survival</u>. Once it is <u>stable</u>, objectives might be centred around <u>growth</u> and <u>maximising profits</u> for reinvestment. If it becomes a <u>large</u>, <u>established</u> business, it might aim to have the <u>largest market share</u> (dominate the market), or to expand into <u>other countries</u>. If it becomes a <u>PLC</u>, increasing <u>shareholder value</u> could become its most important objective.

2) The business environment is <u>dynamic</u> (ever-changing) — for the <u>law</u>, the <u>economy</u>, <u>technology</u> or the expectations of <u>customers</u> may all change. Firms need to be able to <u>keep up</u> with these changes. They can do this by changing their <u>objectives</u>. E.g.

- <u>New legislation</u> — companies may need to adjust their objectives when <u>new laws</u> are introduced. E.g. in 2016, a new <u>living wage</u> was introduced. This affected many companies' <u>profit</u> objectives, as they had to pay <u>higher wages</u>.

- <u>Changes in the economy</u> — e.g. if there's a <u>recession</u>, a company's <u>growth</u> objectives might be <u>put on hold</u> while it concentrates on <u>survival</u>.

- <u>Changes in technology</u> — companies need to <u>keep up to date</u> with new technology, especially if their competitors are using it. They may need to alter their objectives so they spend more money on getting <u>new equipment</u> and <u>training staff</u> rather than investing in <u>growth</u>.

- <u>Environmental expectations</u> — recently people have become more <u>concerned</u> about the <u>impact</u> a business has on the <u>environment</u> — objectives related to environmental impact have become <u>more important</u> for many companies to avoid <u>losing customers</u>.

Businesses Use Objectives to Monitor Success

1) Once a business has set objectives, it can check back after a period of time to see whether those objectives have been <u>achieved</u>. This is a way of <u>measuring success</u>.

2) A <u>common</u> objective to look at is <u>profit</u> — e.g. if the firm met a yearly <u>profit target</u> it's a sign of success.

3) There are <u>loads</u> of ways <u>other than profit</u> to measure success, depending on the firm's objectives. For example, a firm could count the <u>number of employees</u> it has to see if it's met its <u>growth</u> objectives, or look at the <u>value</u> of its <u>shares</u> on the <u>stock market</u> to see if it's met its <u>shareholder value</u> objectives.

Not tripping over my own feet — my daily objective...

PRACTICE QUESTION

Q1 Green Machines is a firm that makes lawnmowers. It's main objective is to maximise its profits.
  a) Explain how Green Machines could monitor whether it has achieved this objective.
  b) Explain one way the firm's objectives may change if the market it's in becomes very competitive.

Stakeholders

A <u>stakeholder</u> is <u>anyone</u> who's affected by a business. Even <u>small businesses</u> may have lots of stakeholders.

Different Stakeholders Have Different Ideas of Success

Different stakeholders are affected by the business in <u>different ways</u>. This means they have different <u>opinions</u> about what makes a firm <u>successful</u> and what its <u>objectives</u> should be. For example:

The <u>owners</u> are the most important stakeholders. They make a <u>profit</u> if the business is successful and <u>decide</u> what happens to the business. In a <u>limited company</u>, the <u>shareholders</u> are the owners (see p.6). Shareholders usually want <u>high dividends</u>, and a <u>high share price</u>.

> Dividends are payments that the shareholders get if the company makes a profit. The more shares a shareholder owns, the higher their dividend will be.

<u>Employees</u> are interested in their <u>job security</u> and <u>promotion prospects</u>. These are improved if the firm is <u>profitable</u> and <u>growing</u>. Employees also want a <u>decent wage</u> and <u>good working conditions</u>. So they may benefit most when objectives are based on <u>profitability</u>, <u>growth</u> and <u>ethics</u>.

A firm buys its <u>raw materials</u> from <u>suppliers</u>. If the firm is profitable and grows they'll need more materials and the supplier will get more business and therefore its income will <u>increase</u>. So suppliers benefit most when the firm sets objectives based on <u>profitability</u> and <u>growth</u>.

The <u>local community</u> where the business is based will suffer if the firm causes <u>noise and pollution</u>. They may gain if the firm provides <u>good jobs</u> and <u>sponsors</u> local activities. If the business <u>employs</u> local people, these employees will then have money to spend in <u>local shops</u>, which is good for the local economy. So the local community may benefit when objectives are based on <u>minimising environmental impacts</u>, <u>ethical considerations</u>, <u>profitability</u> and <u>growth</u>.

The <u>government</u> will receive <u>taxes</u> if the firm makes a <u>profit</u>. They may benefit most when objectives are based on <u>profitability</u>, <u>growth</u>, or <u>job creation</u>.

<u>Customers</u> want <u>high quality</u> products at <u>low prices</u>. They benefit when objectives are based on <u>customer satisfaction</u>.

Stakeholders Influence Objectives to Varying Degrees

1) The <u>owners</u> make the <u>decisions</u> in a firm, so they're they <u>most influential</u> stakeholders.

2) However, they need to consider the interests of <u>other stakeholders</u> when they're setting their objectives.

3) Often, stakeholders will have <u>conflicting opinions</u> about the firm's objectives.

4) The firm may decide to <u>ignore</u> the opinions of some stakeholders, but they'll need to take others into account if they want to <u>survive</u> as a firm. For example:

I thought you said stay colder.

- No business can ignore its <u>customers</u>. If it can't sell its products it won't survive.
- And if a business doesn't have happy <u>workers</u> it may become <u>unproductive</u>.
- But a company may not mind being <u>unpopular</u> in the <u>local community</u> if it sells most of its products somewhere else.

> BUSINESS EXAMPLE

- A <u>restaurant</u> is building a <u>new outlet</u> in Hursleton.
- The owners want the restaurant opened <u>as soon as possible</u> so it can start making an <u>income</u>. However, this would mean working <u>at night</u>, which is <u>noisy</u> and could disturb <u>local residents</u>. The company wants to keep the residents <u>happy</u>, so that they become <u>customers</u>.
- So the company has to balance the interests of <u>both stakeholders</u> (the owners and the local community) to make sure the restaurant is built in a <u>quick</u>, but <u>non-disruptive</u> way.

Stakeholders — vampires are terrified of them...

...but you don't need to be. Just remember that people affected by a business are called stakeholders and they can influence a firm's objectives. But some stakeholders have more power over a business's decisions than others.

Revenue, Costs and Profit

The stuff on this page is really <u>important</u> — it all hinges on one simple sum: <u>profit = revenue – costs</u>.

Revenue *is the Income Earned by a Business*

1) Businesses earn most of their <u>income</u> from <u>selling</u> their products to customers.

2) Revenue can be <u>calculated</u> by multiplying <u>sales</u> (the number of units sold) by the <u>price</u> (the amount the customer pays).

BUSINESS EXAMPLE

> **revenue = sales × price**

> If Britney's Spheres Ltd. sell <u>20 000</u> tennis balls at <u>£2</u> each — their <u>sales revenue</u> will be <u>£40 000</u>.

Costs *are the Expenses Paid Out to Run the Business*

Fixed and Variable Costs

- <u>Fixed</u> costs <u>don't vary</u> with output (the amount a business produces). They <u>have to be paid</u> even if the firm produces <u>nothing</u>. For example, the <u>rent</u>, <u>insurance</u> and <u>fixed salaries</u> for employees such as <u>managers</u>.

- <u>Variable</u> costs are costs that will <u>increase</u> as the firm <u>expands output</u>. For example, the costs of <u>factory labour</u>, <u>raw materials</u> and <u>running machinery</u>.

- Fixed costs are only fixed over a <u>short period</u> of time — an expanding firm's fixed costs will go up.

> **total costs = variable costs + fixed costs**

Average Unit Cost

- Average unit cost is how much <u>each product</u> costs to make.

- To find the average unit cost, divide the <u>total cost</u> by <u>output</u> (number of products made).

> **average unit cost = total cost ÷ output**

- To make a profit the firm must charge a <u>higher price</u> than this.

- Average unit costs usually <u>fall</u> as the firm <u>grows</u>, due to <u>economies of scale</u> (see p.14).

BUSINESS EXAMPLE

> Britney's Spheres Ltd. has an output of 20 000 tennis balls, at a <u>total cost</u> of £30 000. The <u>average unit cost</u> = £30 000 ÷ 20 000 = <u>£1.50 per ball</u>. The selling price should be <u>more than</u> £1.50 per ball.

Businesses Make a Profit *if They Earn More Than They Spend*

<u>Profit</u> (or loss) is the difference between revenue and costs over a <u>period of time</u>.

> **profit = revenue – costs**

BUSINESS EXAMPLE

> Britney's Spheres Ltd. sells <u>20 000</u> tennis balls in a month at <u>£2 each</u>. Over the same month its total costs are <u>£30 000</u>. Profit = (20 000 × £2) – £30 000 = <u>£40 000</u> – £30 000 = £10 000 So the business makes <u>£10 000 profit</u> in the month.

If <u>costs</u> are <u>higher</u> than revenue, the business will make a <u>loss</u> instead of a profit, and the answer to the calculation above will be <u>negative</u>.

> Sounds like a load of balls to me.

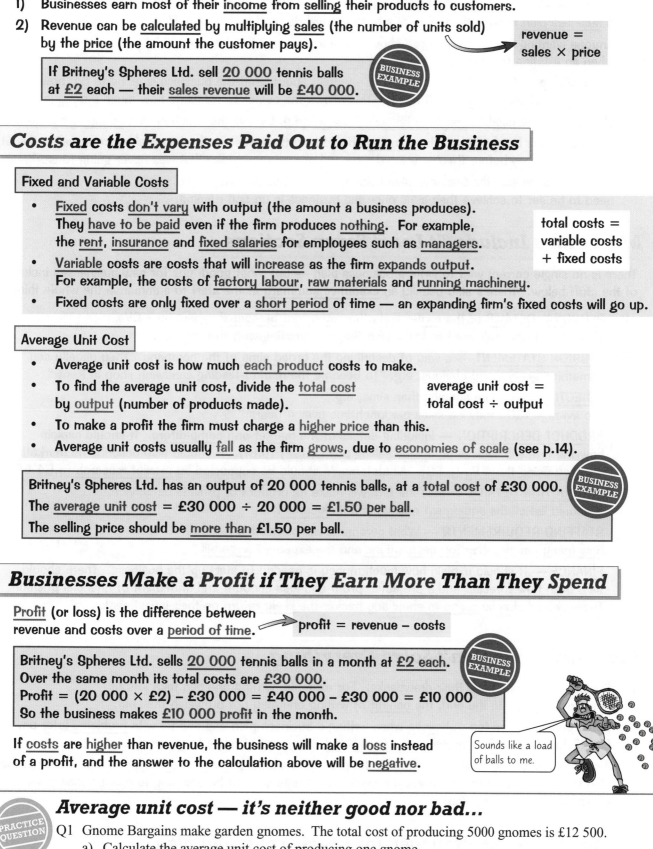

PRACTICE QUESTION

Average unit cost — it's neither good nor bad...

Q1 Gnome Bargains make garden gnomes. The total cost of producing 5000 gnomes is £12 500.
   a) Calculate the average unit cost of producing one gnome.
   b) Each gnome is sold for £7. Calculate the profit Gnome Bargains will make if they sell all 5000 gnomes.

The Business Plan

It's vital that a business has a <u>clear idea</u> of what it's going to do if it wants to be successful — this is where the <u>business plan</u> comes in. You need to know <u>why</u> businesses have them and <u>what</u> they should contain.

The Plan is for the Owner and Financial Backers

1) A <u>business plan</u> is an outline of <u>what</u> a business will do, and <u>how</u> it aims to do it.

2) Anyone wanting to <u>start a business</u> should have a plan, but they're also useful when an <u>existing firm</u> wants to make <u>changes</u>.

3) A business plan forces the owner to <u>think carefully</u> about what the business is <u>going to do</u>, how it will be <u>organised</u> and what <u>resources</u> it needs. This allows the owner to calculate how much <u>money</u> is needed.

4) The plan can be used to <u>convince financial backers</u> (e.g. banks) that the idea is a <u>sound investment</u>.

5) If the business is a <u>bad idea</u>, the <u>planning</u> should help the owner or the financial backers realise this at an <u>early stage</u> — before they've wasted <u>time and money</u> on an idea that was never going to work.

6) For a new business, the business plan helps managers decide what <u>objectives</u> need to be set to achieve their <u>aims</u> once the business is up and running.

Most Plans Include At Least Seven Sections

There is no single <u>correct way</u> to write a business plan — but most good 'uns for new businesses include all of the stuff below. There's also usually an <u>executive summary</u> at the start to summarise the whole thing.

1) <u>PERSONAL DETAILS</u> of the <u>owner</u> and other <u>important personnel</u> — like their <u>CVs</u>. Financial backers will want to know who they are trusting with their money.

2) <u>MISSION STATEMENT</u> — a way of describing the <u>broad aims</u> of the company. They usually say something <u>general and obvious</u>, e.g. "To become the market-leading sandwich shop in Kent."

3) <u>OBJECTIVES</u> are more <u>specific</u> than aims, e.g. "To average 160 sandwich sales per lunchtime over 4 years."

4) <u>PRODUCT DESCRIPTION</u> — including details of the <u>market</u> and <u>competitors</u>. It should explain how the firm will achieve its <u>unique selling point (USP)</u> (p.61). It should also describe its <u>marketing strategy</u> using the <u>4 Ps</u> (p.53). All statements should be supported by <u>market research</u> (p.54-56).

5) <u>PRODUCTION DETAILS</u> — how the firm will make its product or provide its service. It should list all the <u>equipment</u> needed and its <u>location</u>.

6) <u>STAFFING REQUIREMENTS</u> — What <u>personnel</u> will be needed — how many people, their <u>job descriptions</u> and the expected <u>wage bill</u>.

All these financial bits and bobs are covered in Section 6.

7) <u>FINANCE</u> — It should explain how much <u>money</u> is needed to <u>start up</u> the business. There should be a <u>cash flow</u> forecast and a projected <u>profit and loss account</u> and <u>statement of financial position</u>. There should also be <u>ratios</u> to show any backer the <u>likely return</u> on their investment.

Business Plans Don't Solve Everything

1) Business plans can have their drawbacks. For example, writing one can take lots of <u>time</u> and <u>money</u>. In the end, the <u>benefit</u> of writing one may not outweigh the <u>cost</u>.

2) Some people will be too <u>optimistic</u> when writing a business plan and end up with <u>problems</u> later on. E.g. if they don't <u>sell</u> as much as they <u>predicted</u>, they may struggle to <u>pay their bills</u>.

3) Also, managers may stick <u>too tightly</u> to the plan. If something <u>unexpected</u> happens that wasn't in the plan (e.g. a new competitor enters the market), managers might be unwilling to <u>change</u> their plans, which could lead to <u>problems</u>.

Fear not, Mrs Bank Manager, for I have a cunning plan...

The best laid business plans might not stop a fledgling business from going under — but anyone starting a firm without one would need improbable amounts of luck to survive. In short, plans are important. Learn.

Location

Sometimes, success in business is all about being in the right place. When a firm chooses where it's going to locate, it usually has to compromise between producing where it's cheapest and being where it would generate the most income. There are other factors which are also important — depending on the business.

Location is Influenced by Five Main Factors

Suppose a new start-up company Granite King are looking for a location for their new kitchen worktop manufacturing business. They'll want to think about these things...

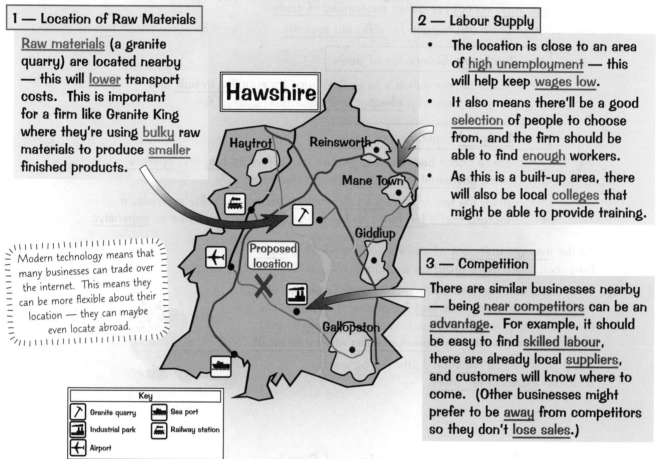

1 — Location of Raw Materials

Raw materials (a granite quarry) are located nearby — this will lower transport costs. This is important for a firm like Granite King where they're using bulky raw materials to produce smaller finished products.

Modern technology means that many businesses can trade over the internet. This means they can be more flexible about their location — they can maybe even locate abroad.

Hawshire

Haytrot

Reinsworth

Mane Town

Giddiup

Proposed location

Gallopston

Key
- Granite quarry
- Sea port
- Industrial park
- Railway station
- Airport

2 — Labour Supply

- The location is close to an area of high unemployment — this will help keep wages low.
- It also means there'll be a good selection of people to choose from, and the firm should be able to find enough workers.
- As this is a built-up area, there will also be local colleges that might be able to provide training.

3 — Competition

There are similar businesses nearby — being near competitors can be an advantage. For example, it should be easy to find skilled labour, there are already local suppliers, and customers will know where to come. (Other businesses might prefer to be away from competitors so they don't lose sales.)

Other businesses might consider these factors:

4 — Location of the Market

- Some firms pay more to transport their finished products than their raw materials. These types of firms find it cheapest to locate near to their customers.
- Some services (e.g. dentists) locate where people can easily get to them.
- Firms that sell products across the world may set up production sites in countries where they have a large market. This reduces transport costs and means they won't have to pay import taxes in these countries.

5 — Cost

- The cost of labour varies in different countries. Many large firms have call centres and factories in places such as India or China where wages are lower.
- How much the firm can afford to spend on renting or buying will affect where it is — some areas are much more expensive than others. E.g. it costs a lot more to rent a shop on the high street than it does in a quieter area of town.
- Sometimes the government gives grants or tax breaks for firms who locate in areas of high unemployment, which lowers their total expenditure.

Location of the market — it's on the High Street, mate...

Make sure you learn the five factors that can influence where a business decides to locate. As a bit of fun, think of a few businesses and decide what location location location factors would be important for them.

Expanding Businesses

There are lots of different ways that firms can <u>expand</u> (these are covered on the next two pages). But first you need to understand one of the <u>main benefits</u> of being a big firm, as well as some of the <u>drawbacks</u>.

Larger Firms Benefit from Economies of Scale

1) <u>Larger firms</u> generally make <u>more products</u> and have <u>more money</u> than smaller firms.

2) Being larger means that the <u>average unit cost</u> of each product <u>falls</u> — these <u>reductions in cost</u> are called <u>economies of scale</u>.

3) Economies of scale can happen for <u>different reasons</u>. You need to know about <u>two</u> of them:

> **1 — <u>Purchasing</u> Economies of Scale**
> - These happen when a large firm <u>buys its supplies in bulk</u> and so gets them at a <u>cheaper unit price</u> than a small firm.

> **2 — <u>Technical</u> Economies of Scale**
> - These occur because a large firm can afford to <u>buy</u> and <u>operate</u> more <u>advanced machinery</u> than smaller firms.
> - Also, the law of <u>increased dimensions</u> means that, for example, a factory that's <u>ten times as big</u> will be <u>less than</u> ten times as <u>expensive</u>.

4) As the <u>average unit cost</u> of making each product is <u>lower</u>, firms can make <u>more profit</u> on each item they sell.

5) Also, lower average unit costs mean larger firms can afford to <u>charge</u> their customers <u>less</u> for products than smaller firms can. This may make customers <u>more likely</u> to <u>buy</u> their products, leading to <u>increased sales</u> and <u>more profit</u>.

6) The profits can be <u>reinvested</u> into the business so it can <u>expand even more</u>.

Geoffrey, with regret, you're fired.

Freida! I said <u>expand</u> the business!

There are also Diseconomies of Scale

It's not all good news for large firms though — growth brings with it the risks of <u>diseconomies of scale</u>. These are areas where growth can lead to <u>increases</u> in <u>average unit costs</u>. For example:

1) The <u>bigger</u> the firm, the <u>harder</u> and <u>more expensive</u> it is to <u>manage</u> it properly.

2) Bigger firms have <u>more people</u>, so it can be harder to <u>communicate</u> within the company. Decisions <u>take time</u> to reach the whole workforce, and workers at the bottom of the hierarchy feel <u>insignificant</u>. Workers can get <u>demotivated</u>, which may cause <u>productivity</u> to go down.

See pages 42-43 for more on hierarchies.

3) The <u>production process</u> may become <u>more complex</u> and more difficult to <u>coordinate</u>. For example, <u>different departments</u> may end up working on very <u>similar</u> projects without knowing.

Economies of scale — don't diss them...

Q1 Lucky Dice are a company that make board games. They have recently expanded by building an extension to double the size of their factory and by hiring ten more staff members.
  a) Explain how the factory extension could lead to technical economies of scale.
  b) Explain why the business expansion might mean Lucky Dice charge less for their games.
  c) Explain one way that the business expansion might cause problems for Lucky Dice.

Internal Expansion

There are two main types of expansion — internal and external. First up it's internal expansion. Lucky you.

Internal Expansion is Low Risk but can be Slow

1) Internal expansion (or organic growth) is when a business grows by expanding its own activities.

2) Internal expansion is good as it's relatively inexpensive. Also, it generally means the firm expands by doing more of what it's already good at — making its existing products. So it's less likely to go wrong.

3) The firm grows slowly, so it's easier to make sure quality doesn't suffer and new staff are trained well.

4) The problem is that it can take a long time to achieve growth — some owners don't want to wait this long to start making more money.

5) Here are three methods of organic growth:

E-commerce

1) This is where a firm sells products via the internet.

2) Lots of people can buy products from the firm, even if they're not near a shop. So the business has access to a much larger market.

3) It's cheaper than setting up and running a new store — the firm doesn't have to pay for rent and won't have to hire as many staff.

4) But technology (e.g. websites or apps) has to be regularly updated. And any technical problems can cause customers to become unsatisfied.

Opening New Stores

1) This is fairly low risk. If the new store operates in a similar way to the existing stores, it should be a success, and so the business can increase its sales.

2) However, opening a store means lots of extra costs, e.g. rent and staff pay. The company needs to make sure it can afford these new costs.

Outsourcing

1) A business could pay another firm to carry out tasks it could do itself — this is outsourcing.

2) The outsourcing firm might be able to do tasks more quickly, cheaply or to a higher standard than the business can do itself.

3) But outsourcing means the business loses some control over parts of its operations. And the firm they've outsourced to might not prioritise their work if they've also got other customers.

4) The business could also get a bad reputation if the firm it outsources to has poor standards.

Franchising Can be Classed as Organic Growth

1) Franchising is where a company expands by giving other firms the right to sell its products (or use its trademarks) in return for a fee or a percentage of the profits. Franchising is slightly different to the methods of growth shown above as it involves new businesses being set up.

2) The product manufacturers are known as franchisors and the firms selling their products are franchisees.

3) Some franchises trade under the name of the franchisee but advertise that they sell a particular manufacturer's products. Car dealerships are an example of this type of franchise.

4) Branded franchises go one stage further. The franchisee buys the right to trade under the name of the franchisor. Most of the big firms in the fast-food industry are this type of franchise.

5) Franchising has many advantages. It increases a franchisor's income (as it gets money from the franchisee), and it increases the market share and brand awareness of products. It also means the firm doesn't have the usual risks and costs of running a new outlet — the franchisee is responsible for these.

6) However, if a franchisee has poor standards the franchisor's brand could get a bad reputation.

Food babies — just another example of internal expansion...

Franchises are a bit weird — one company disguised as another. Make sure you understand them before you go on.

External Expansion

External expansion means expanding by working with other businesses. External expansion is faster than internal expansion, but can be difficult for all the businesses involved.

Mergers and Takeovers are Two Ways to Expand Externally

1) A merger is when two firms join together to form a new (but larger) firm.

2) A takeover is when an existing firm expands by buying more than half the shares in another firm.

3) External expansion means that the business grows much more quickly than with internal expansion.

4) There are four basic ways a firm can merge with or take over other firms.
   Each way has its own advantages:

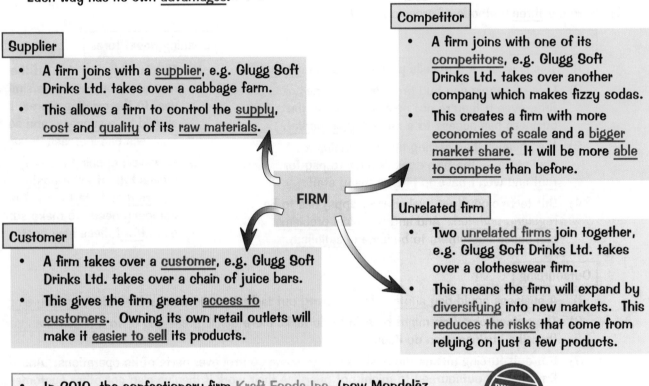

Supplier
- A firm joins with a supplier, e.g. Glugg Soft Drinks Ltd. takes over a cabbage farm.
- This allows a firm to control the supply, cost and quality of its raw materials.

Competitor
- A firm joins with one of its competitors, e.g. Glugg Soft Drinks Ltd. takes over another company which makes fizzy sodas.
- This creates a firm with more economies of scale and a bigger market share. It will be more able to compete than before.

FIRM

Customer
- A firm takes over a customer, e.g. Glugg Soft Drinks Ltd. takes over a chain of juice bars.
- This gives the firm greater access to customers. Owning its own retail outlets will make it easier to sell its products.

Unrelated firm
- Two unrelated firms join together, e.g. Glugg Soft Drinks Ltd. takes over a clotheswear firm.
- This means the firm will expand by diversifying into new markets. This reduces the risks that come from relying on just a few products.

- In 2010, the confectionery firm Kraft Foods Inc. (now Mondelēz International) bought enough shares to take over its competitor Cadbury.
- By taking over Cadbury, Kraft Foods Inc. became the largest seller of chocolate and confectionery in the world.
- Buying Cadbury also meant that Kraft Foods Inc. immediately had good market shares in parts of the world where it hadn't sold much before.

BUSINESS EXAMPLE

Doreen, we need backup. We've got another student-lamppost merger.

Mergers and Takeovers Don't Always Go Smoothly

1) Less than half of all takeovers and mergers are successful. It's very hard to make two different businesses work as one. Management styles often differ between firms — the employees of one firm may be used to one company culture and not be motivated by the style used in the other.

2) Mergers and takeovers can also create bad feeling. Often a firm agrees to be taken over, but sometimes the takeover bid is hostile and unpopular.

3) Mergers and takeovers often lead to cost-cutting. This may mean making lots of people redundant, so they can lead to tension and uncertainty among workers.

Hitchcock Takeover Consultancy — Dial M for Merger...

Loads of new stuff to learn here — but I don't reckon any of it's too tricky. Make sure you know how businesses can expand by mergers or takeovers, and the advantages and disadvantages of expanding in these ways.

Case Study — Business in the Real World

There's a lot going on in this Section — types of business, all those equations for costs and profit, growing a business... My head's spinning. Here's a nice case study to help you get to grips with it. Lovely.

Business Report: Business in the Real World

Scoop of the Day

Sophie is the owner of Scoop of the Day — a café that sells ice cream sundaes. The café is located on the high street of Ladwellington, where it costs £1500 per month in rent. For the last four years, profits have grown 10% each year. Now, Sophie has decided to open a second café in the neighbouring town of Worthbury. At the same time, she has decided to incorporate her business to make it a private limited company.

Sophie looks at three possible locations for the new café. A summary of her research is shown in the table below:

Location	Cost of rent per month	Description
12 Market Street	£1900	The building is on a busy shopping street. There are two other cafés on the street which sell hot drinks and pastries. The other shops are mainly clothes shops.
Mega Mall	£2500	The pitch is in the food court of a busy shopping centre. The surrounding shops are all food outlets, including a shop selling cookies and another selling frozen yoghurt.
Sutcliff Park	£1650	The building is next to a park popular with families. There are no other cafés in the area. During the summer there is an ice cream van by the park gate.

Case Study Questions

Time for a few questions to see what you've learnt. Don't worry if you find them tricky to begin with — just go back and have another read through of the section.

1) State what sector of the market Scoop of the Day is in.
2) Explain one possible reason why Sophie has decided to make her business a private limited company.
3) Discuss one possible benefit and one possible risk for Sophie in choosing to expand her business.
4) Recommend which location Sophie should choose for her new café. Give reasons for your answer.

I scream, you scream — that's just case studies, I'm afraid...

Well, there you go. Your first case study, all done and dusted. Now time to check the freezer for some ice cream...

Revision Summary

Well, here we are. The final page of Section 1. What a section it's been, and it's not quite over yet. Before you run off, there's just time to have a go at a few questions.

1) Define the term 'goods'.
2) Describe the difference between needs and wants.
3) Give an example of a type of business that you would find in:
    a) the primary sector,   b) the secondary sector,   c) the tertiary sector.
4) What is enterprise?
5) Describe two reasons why someone might decide to become an entrepreneur.
6) State two qualities that you would expect an entrepreneur to have.
7) Name the four factors of production.
8) What is meant by the term 'opportunity cost'?
9) True or false? A sole trader is responsible for all the debts of a business.
10) What is meant by the term 'limited liability'?
11) State two types of business ownership structure that have limited liability.
12) Describe one difference between a private limited company and a public limited company.
13) Give two disadvantages of being a public limited company rather than a private limited company.
14) What is a not-for-profit organisation?
15) Why might a social enterprise have more control over how much money it can spend on projects compared to a charity?
16) Describe two aims a business might have.
17) Describe the difference between business aims and objectives.
18) Explain how the objectives of a start-up business are likely to be different from that of a larger, more established business.
19) Describe what is meant by the term 'stakeholder'.
20) State four possible stakeholders in a business.
21) State the equation that can be used to calculate revenue using sales figures and price.
22) Describe what you would expect to happen to a firm's variable costs if it expanded its output.
23) Give one example of a fixed cost a business could have.
24) State one advantage of writing a business plan.
25) Outline the main sections of a business plan.
26) State one disadvantage of writing a business plan.
27) List five factors that may influence the location chosen for a business.
28) What are purchasing economies of scale?
29) State two diseconomies of scale a business might experience as it grows.
30) What is organic growth?
31) Give one advantage and one disadvantage of expanding by e-commerce.
32) Describe how a business can use outsourcing to expand.
33) What is franchising?
34) State one advantage and one disadvantage of franchising to a franchisor.
35) Describe the difference between takeovers and mergers.
36) Explain two disadvantages of external expansion.

Employment and the Law

The next two pages are all about the law. First up it's employment law and then some health and safety law. The most important thing here is the effect of the different laws rather than the ins and outs of them.

Businesses Have to Pay Staff a Minimum Amount

1) There are laws about the minimum amount employers have to pay their staff.

2) Workers aged 24 and under but of school leaving age have to be paid the National Minimum Wage (the exact amount depends on the age of the worker and the type of work). Workers aged 25 and over have to be paid the National Living Wage — which is slightly more than the National Minimum Wage.

- The National Minimum Wage and National Living Wage mean that companies can't cut their costs by paying workers less than the legal minimum. If they do, they're breaking the law.
- If a company doesn't pay its workers enough, it could be given large fines. It could also get bad publicity, and consumers might stop using the business.
- Companies sometimes argue that the National Minimum Wage and National Living Wage increase costs. These increased costs can lead to increased prices, meaning a possible fall in sales and a reduced income for the firm.
- The National Minimum Wage and National Living Wage can have benefits for companies though — they can lead to better motivated staff and increased productivity.

The National Living Wage and the National Minimum Wage are usually increased each year.

Businesses Can't Discriminate

1) Recruitment procedures must not discriminate against anyone because of, for example, their religion, gender, race, age, sexual orientation or because of disabilities. This is covered by the Equality Act 2010.

2) Apart from recruitment, the other main equal opportunities issue covered by the Equality Act 2010 is pay — all employees must be paid the same if they do the same job (or work of equal value) for the same employer.

3) If a company is found to have discriminated against someone, they'll have to pay compensation.

4) If any employee in a company is accused of discrimination, the company could also be held responsible. So companies need to take reasonable steps to prevent discrimination within the workplace — such as staff training and writing company policies about equal rights.

The Workplace Needs to be Safe

1) Health and safety legislation helps to make sure that risks to people at work are properly controlled.

- The Health and Safety at Work Act of 1974 requires all employers and their employees to take responsibility for health and safety.
- Firms need to carry out risk assessments to identify possible dangers.
- They need to take reasonable steps to reduce the risks. For example, accident books need to be kept, and first-aiders trained. All staff must receive health and safety training. Health and safety equipment must also be provided — e.g. hard hats on building sites.

Health and safety laws protect visitors to a firm (e.g. customers) as well as the workers.

2) A safe working environment should mean fewer accidents, and so fewer injuries. And hopefully it means a more productive workforce too — since people should need less time off work to recover.

3) It could also encourage people to apply to work for a company if they know they're safe to work for.

4) Following health and safety laws can be expensive — e.g. paying for staff to go on safety courses.

5) But businesses that don't follow health and safety laws can be prosecuted, fined and even closed down.

6) They may also have to pay compensation to anyone who's injured, and could get bad publicity.

The law is fragile — careful not to break it...

Making sure all business activities are within the law can take time and be expensive, but all firms need to do it.

Consumer Law

There are laws restricting how firms sell their products — the aim is to protect the consumer.
If these laws weren't in place, some businesses might be tempted to be a bit dishonest.
Like the time I bought a new TV that turned out to be an egg-whisk. Oh, come on — we've all done it.

The Consumer Rights Act Sets Conditions for Products

The Consumer Rights Act 2015 covers how goods and services can be sold.
It basically states that goods should meet three criteria:

1 — The product should be fit for its purpose

The product has to do the job it was designed for — if you buy a
bucket, say, it's not much use if it leaks water out of the bottom.

2 — The product should match its description

...and it's magic and fires lasers and does your maths homework and makes you really attractive...

* The way a business describes a product it's selling is called a 'trade description'. It's illegal for a retailer to give a false trade description.
* This includes the size or quantity of the product, the materials it's made from, and its properties.
* It's also illegal to claim that a product has been endorsed or approved by a person or an organisation unless it really has been.

3 — The product should be of satisfactory quality

* This means that the product should be well made — it shouldn't fall apart after a couple of uses.
* It also means that it shouldn't cause other problems for the buyer — e.g. a fridge should keep food cold, but it shouldn't make a noise like a jet plane at the same time.

If products don't meet the legal requirements, customers can ask for their money back,
a repair or a replacement.

Consumer Laws Affect Businesses

1) If a business breaks consumer law it is faced with the cost and inconvenience of having to refund the customer, or repair or replace their item.
2) The case could even end up in court if the customer is unhappy with the business's response about their item (which costs the business even more if the customer wins the case).
3) As well as being expensive, breaking consumer law can harm the reputation of the business, which could lead to a reduction in sales.
4) So businesses have to be very careful when selling products and services to their customers.
5) They need to make sure they train their staff properly, so they sell products accurately and understand what a customer's rights are if they are unhappy with a product.

Consume a law — I'm told it tastes like chocolate...

PRACTICE QUESTION

Q1 Martine buys a new pencil case from a company's website. The product description online says it's suitable for standard stationery needs, and should arrive within three days of purchase.
When the pencil case arrives, Martine discovers it is too short to fit a normal sized pen.
Explain one way in which the company selling the pencil case has broken consumer law.

Technology and Business

Turns out my carrier pigeon service isn't the most up-to-date way of communicating with people. Who knew?

Technology has Changed the way Businesses Operate

1) Developments in information and communications technology (ICT) have improved how businesses work. They often make processes faster — e.g. because computers can do jobs more quickly than before or because people can communicate with each other more easily. They can also lead to reduced costs in the long term — e.g. because fewer man-hours are needed to carry out tasks.

   ICT includes loads of things, such as computers, phone networks and the internet.

2) However, adapting to new technology can be very expensive. For example, a business may have to buy equipment or train staff to use new computer systems. They may also need to hire staff with the skills to use the new technology.

E-Commerce Means Buying and Selling Online

There's lots more about e-commerce on p.67-68.

1) E-commerce is using the internet to buy or sell products.
2) Many firms now have websites where customers can buy their products.
3) E-commerce means that firms can reach wider markets compared to just having traditional shops — e.g. a small business in Dorset could end up selling products to someone in New Zealand.
4) Firms have had to adapt to e-commerce as it's become more important. For example, they've had to build websites, employ IT specialists and develop systems to distribute products to online customers.

Firms can Communicate Digitally with Stakeholders

A stakeholder is anyone who is affected by a business (see p.10).

There are many ways firms can use technology to communicate with their stakeholders:

SOCIAL MEDIA: Companies are using social media more and more to communicate — e.g. to advertise their products to customers, to provide customer service or to promote local events to a community.

WEBSITES: Websites are a great way to communicate with customers — e.g. by posting blogs or providing customer service (such as FAQs). Websites can also be used to publish reports to shareholders.

EMAIL: Email is a very quick way of communicating with stakeholders, either on a personal level (e.g. to respond to a customer query) or on a bigger scale (e.g. to tell all employees they can go home early).

MOBILE APPS: These are programs used on mobile devices, such as smartphones or tablets. They are usually used by firms to communicate with customers, for example by giving information about where stores are located, the products the company sells and any special offers.

LIVE CHATS: Live chats are an instant messaging service. They have many uses — e.g. employees can use them to talk to each other from different locations, or customers can use them to speak with a customer services advisor via the internet.

Looks like a great web site you've got there, Ethel.

VIDEO CALLS: Employees who work for the same business in different locations may use video calling to hold meetings, rather than travelling to meet up. This can also be a good way for businesses to communicate with important shareholders, who may all live in different places.

Companies need to adapt the way they communicate with stakeholders so they stay competitive. For example, if a company's competitors are communicating with customers using apps or on social media, then the company should also consider doing these things.

An app a day keeps the business doctor away...

Customers expect businesses to adapt to new ways of communication. Nowadays people are used to being able to find information instantly, at any time. Businesses that don't change will probably have a hard time surviving.

Ethical Considerations

There are lots of things a business can do to make sure it's being fair and honest. Many stakeholders are concerned about how businesses behave towards others, and whether they act in an ethical way.

Ethical Issues Have Become Important for Businesses

1) Ethics are the moral principles of right and wrong.

2) Many firms have their own ethical policies. This means they've developed ways of working that stakeholders think are fair and honest.

3) The ways that UK firms treat employees and suppliers in other countries raises many ethical issues.

- In some countries, it's not illegal for people to work very long hours for very low pay. Some firms set up factories in these countries to reduce their labour costs — many people think this is unethical if it exploits workers from foreign countries.

- Businesses can write codes of conduct for any factories they have overseas. This helps to ensure that the workers are treated ethically. For example, they can put limits on the number of hours somebody can work each week so they don't get too tired. They could carry out checks to make sure the code is being followed.

- Firms that buy raw materials from developing countries can choose to buy from Fair Trade sources — this means people in developing countries who produce the goods (e.g. cocoa farmers) are paid a fair price so they can earn decent wages.

4) Businesses need to treat their employees in the UK ethically too. E.g. businesses should reward staff fairly, keep personal details about staff private and provide a comfortable working environment.

5) Treating people well isn't the only ethical issue for a business. For example, when promoting products, firms have to follow codes of practice — they can't be dishonest or slate other brands in adverts (although competing products can now be compared in a fair way). Some products can't be advertised at all — e.g. cigarette adverts are banned on health grounds.

6) Firms are also under pressure to carry out product development in an ethical way — this means using non-toxic materials, paying close attention to safety, and not using animal testing.

Acting Ethically can have Benefits and Drawbacks

1) Ethical policies can be costly for a firm. For example, by treating workers fairly and making sure they are all paid a fair wage, a business is likely to have higher labour costs than if they didn't work ethically.

2) Also, if a firm is committed to using ethically sourced materials (e.g. Fair Trade products) they may find it more difficult to find suppliers and have to pay a higher price for their materials.

3) These increased costs mean that a firm doesn't make as much profit on each item that it sells. It could put its prices up so that it makes more profit per item, but higher prices might lead to lower sales (so the business still ends up with less profit).

4) However, despite potentially making less profit, many firms are still keen to work ethically.

5) Firms might change their marketing to emphasise the fact that they have strong ethical policies. For example, the Co-op advertises all its chocolate as Fair Trade produced. By advertising its ethical policies, a business might gain customers and increase its profits — there are plenty of people who think that ethical practices are more important than price.

6) Acting ethically can have a positive effect on other stakeholders as well. For example, some shareholders will be more likely to invest in a firm if it has shown that it behaves ethically. Treating staff ethically can mean workers are more motivated, which should make the firm more productive.

No animals were harmed in the making of this page...

...but several writers were prodded with forks. Not really — CGP is an ethical business. Ethical policies can reduce profits, but there's also plenty of demand for ethical goods.

Environmental Influences

Being a "green" business involves more than just buying a pot of green paint and a paintbrush...

Businesses Can Reduce Their Impact on the Environment

All businesses can have an impact on the environment. They produce waste, lots of which ends up in landfills. They can also cause traffic congestion in the area where they're based if staff, customers and delivery lorries are driving there. Factories, cars and lorries can also cause air, noise and water pollution.

Luckily, there are steps a business can take to reduce these impacts on the environment:

- Companies can reduce the amount of packaging on their products. They can also recycle things such as delivery boxes, or unwanted goods. These things mean that less waste goes to landfill.
- Companies can dispose of hazardous waste carefully so that it doesn't pollute land or water.
- Companies can encourage car share schemes so that they reduce traffic caused by their staff driving to work. They can also support cycle to work schemes, where they help employees to buy bikes.
- To help reduce air pollution, a business can buy more efficient machinery that is less polluting.
- Noise pollution can be a big problem for some firms, such as those in the construction industry. To reduce noise pollution, they can buy quieter machinery, or put up sound barriers or insulation.

Businesses can Aim to be More Sustainable

1) Being sustainable means working in a way that doesn't damage the Earth for future generations.
2) People are worried that the combined impact of global businesses is damaging the Earth at the moment:

- RESOURCE DEPLETION — Many resources used by businesses are non-renewable (e.g. coal and oil). If these resources run out, there's no way we can replace them.
- GLOBAL WARMING — Many industries release carbon dioxide (and other chemicals) into the atmosphere. Carbon dioxide is also released when power stations generate electricity. The rise of carbon dioxide (and other 'greenhouse gases') in the atmosphere is contributing to the Earth's climate becoming warmer. The consequences of this could include icecaps melting, sea levels rising, more flooding... which could have knock-on effects for plant and animal life (including us).

3) Many firms are now working hard to make sure their operations are more sustainable. For example, they're using more renewable energy resources (such as wind and solar power), vehicles and machinery that produce less carbon dioxide and electrical goods that are more energy efficient.

> BUSINESS EXAMPLE
>
> 1) In 2007, Marks and Spencer launched Plan A — a business plan to reduce its environmental impact and improve its ethics.
> 2) They started doing things like designing buildings that wasted less energy and used more sustainable materials.
> 3) By 2014, Marks and Spencer's global operations were carbon neutral — this means that, overall, the business doesn't add any carbon dioxide to the atmosphere.

There are Pros and Cons to Being Environmentally Friendly

1) As people become more aware of environmental issues, consumers are changing their buying decisions — people are now buying more "environmentally friendly" products.
2) Taking environmental issues seriously can give firms a competitive advantage — a "green image" can attract new customers and increase sales.
3) However, buying new equipment and developing new processes in order to be more sustainable can be expensive. Firms have to weigh up the benefits against the negative effect it could have on their profits.

Traffic congestion? You'll need more than a tissue to fix that...

Businesses can't afford to ignore environmental issues — firms that do may find themselves losing customers.

Unemployment and Consumer Spending

Businesses can be affected by <u>how many people</u> are <u>employed</u> and what their <u>incomes</u> are.

Unemployment is a Big Problem

People are <u>unemployed</u> when they're able to work but can't find a job. The <u>level of employment</u> (the number of people in work) changes over time, and this can have a <u>big effect</u> on businesses.

1) Unemployment means the economy as a whole produces <u>less output</u> than if everyone was employed. So <u>everyone</u> suffers from unemployment — in theory at least.

2) UK unemployment was very high in <u>2010</u> — around 2.5 million. In 2016, this had fallen to about 1.6 million.

3) Some <u>firms</u> can actually <u>benefit</u> from unemployment. They may be able to pay <u>lower wages</u> if there are lots of unemployed people <u>desperate</u> for a job. It can also mean they can <u>fill jobs</u> without any difficulty. In areas of <u>high unemployment</u>, the government may even give <u>grants</u> to businesses who open and provide jobs in the area.

4) But there can also be <u>big problems</u> for businesses when there are high levels of unemployment. Less employment means lots of people have <u>less money</u> to spend. This can lead to a <u>lack of demand</u> for products from the unemployed, so sales can <u>fall</u>.

5) It may also be a problem if businesses hire people who have been unemployed for a while — people may <u>lose skills</u> while they're unemployed, so businesses may need to <u>retrain</u> them.

Changes in Income can Affect Businesses

Over time, the <u>price</u> of goods and services can change, and so can the amount that people <u>earn</u> (their income). But they don't necessarily change at the <u>same rate</u>.

If prices rise at a <u>faster</u> rate than income...

- People will have to spend a <u>greater proportion</u> of their income on <u>needs</u> — such as <u>rent</u>, <u>food</u> and <u>electricity bills</u>.

- So they'll have <u>less money</u> left to spend on <u>wants</u>, such as going to the <u>cinema</u>, or buying new <u>shoes</u> — the <u>demand</u> for these products will <u>go down</u>.

- This means businesses that provide <u>wants</u> will <u>suffer</u> — their <u>sales</u> are likely to <u>go down</u>, leading to <u>lower profits</u>. They could <u>lower their prices</u> to increase demand again, but this is still likely to lead to <u>lower profits</u>.

- However, some businesses will <u>benefit</u> if people's incomes are relatively low. Stores selling goods at <u>discount</u> prices are likely to see <u>sales go up</u> as more customers will be making an effort to buy things as <u>cheaply</u> as they can.

If prices are rising at a faster rate than income, income is said to be going down in 'real terms'.

If prices rise at a <u>slower</u> rate than income...

- People will be spending a <u>smaller proportion</u> of their income on <u>needs</u>. This means they'll have <u>more money</u> to spend on <u>wants</u>, and the <u>demand</u> for these goods and services will <u>go up</u>.

- Businesses providing <u>wants</u> will see an <u>increase</u> in <u>sales</u> and their <u>profits</u> are likely to <u>increase</u>.

- Stores selling goods at <u>discount</u> prices may see their <u>sales and profit go down</u> as people start worrying <u>less</u> about getting things for the cheapest possible price.

Protect yourself from falling prices — wear a hard hat...

Q1 George owns a fine dining restaurant. Explain how his sales might be affected if:
    a) Income is rising at a faster rate than prices.
    b) Prices are rising at a faster rate than income.

Interest Rates

Most businesses <u>borrow</u> money to finance their activities. The amount of money they have to pay back depends on the <u>interest rate</u>. <u>Consumers</u> are also affected by interest rates, so this is an important topic.

Interest is Added to Loans and Savings

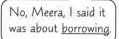

No, Meera, I said it was about <u>borrowing</u>.

1) When you <u>borrow</u> money, you usually have to pay it back with <u>interest</u> — this means that you pay back <u>more</u> than you borrowed.

2) If you <u>save</u> money, you <u>earn</u> interest — the amount of money in your savings account will <u>increase</u> over time.

- The amount of interest you pay or earn depends on the <u>interest rate</u> — it's usually given as a percentage. The <u>higher</u> the interest rate, the <u>more</u> you pay or earn.

- In the UK, the <u>Bank of England</u> sets the <u>base rate</u> of interest — most other interest rates are linked to this. The base rate <u>fluctuates</u> (goes up and down) depending on how good the <u>economy</u> is.

Low Interest Rates Lead to Increased Spending

1) When the interest rate is <u>cut</u>, it's <u>cheaper</u> to <u>borrow</u> money. But you get <u>less interest</u> when you <u>save</u> money at a bank.

2) When rates are <u>low</u>, firms and consumers <u>borrow more</u> and <u>save less</u>.

3) Consumers have <u>more money</u> to spend, so <u>demand</u> for goods and services <u>goes up</u>. This means that firms are likely to make <u>more profit</u> and may need to <u>increase output</u>.

4) Firms that borrow money to finance their spending (e.g. by using <u>overdrafts</u> and <u>loans</u>) will have <u>smaller</u> interest repayments, so they have more money available to spend on <u>other parts</u> of the business. They may also choose to <u>borrow more</u> while interest rates are low, e.g. if they want to grow the business.

High Interest Rates Lead to Decreased Spending

1) <u>Increases</u> in interest rates have the <u>opposite</u> effect to cuts — <u>borrowing</u> money becomes more <u>expensive</u>, but <u>savers</u> get <u>better returns</u> on their investments.

2) Firms and consumers will have <u>less</u> money available to spend — they'll be paying higher rates on money they've borrowed. They're also likely to be trying to <u>save more</u>, in order to take advantage of <u>higher returns</u>.

3) This <u>reduces demand</u> for products, so firms often <u>sell less</u> and their <u>profits</u> may <u>go down</u>.

4) It may also mean that firms can't <u>afford</u> to <u>pay</u> everyone who works for them — so some people may be made <u>redundant</u>, and <u>unemployment</u> may go up.

As revision increases, my interest rate goes down...

Interest rates can be tricky to get your head round. They're like a see-saw — if interest rates go down, spending goes up. If interest rates go up, spending goes down. Have another read to make sure you know why this happens.

Competition

The business world isn't one of those friendly 'it's the taking part that counts' types of competition. Oh, no. Rival businesses will work <u>as hard as they can</u> to <u>beat</u> their <u>competitors</u>.

A Market can be a Place, a Product or a Group of People

The word <u>market</u> can mean <u>three</u> slightly different things:

1) A <u>place</u> where goods are traded between customers and suppliers. A village market square seems pretty different from an internet shopping website — but they're both examples of markets.

2) Trade in a particular <u>type of product</u>, e.g. the oil market.

3) The potential <u>customers</u> for a product, e.g. the age 18–25 market.

Competitors Sell the Same Products in the Same Market

A <u>competitive market</u> is one where there are a <u>large number of producers</u> selling to a <u>large number of consumers</u>. Operating in a competitive market can have a number of <u>effects</u> on a business:

- In a competitive market, nobody is powerful enough to dictate <u>prices</u>. If a firm charges <u>too much</u> then consumers will <u>go elsewhere</u> — this forces producers to be <u>efficient</u>.

- Firms need to try to convince customers that their product is <u>better</u> than their rivals'. This can be <u>costly</u> for firms. E.g. they might need to spend money on <u>developing high quality products</u>, training staff in good <u>after-sales service</u>, or funding <u>promotions</u> to persuade customers to buy their products.

- Firms will rush to fill any <u>gap in the market</u> — supplying a previously unmet consumer need. This results in firms spending lots of money <u>developing new products</u>.

- However, lots of competition means that sometimes all the firms end up making the <u>same product</u>. This means that the only competition is over the <u>selling price</u> of the item — this drives down prices and reduces each firm's <u>profits</u>. If each firm makes smaller profits there may be <u>less money</u> available to develop <u>new and better</u> products.

Some Businesses Face Very Little or No Competition

1) When a business creates a <u>brand new</u> product, initially it won't have any competition. Anyone who wants the product will have to buy it from <u>this business</u>. This will continue until <u>other businesses</u> start selling <u>similar products</u>.

> When a business creates a new product, it may take out a patent. This means other businesses can't copy their idea for a set period of time, and keeps competition low.

2) Some businesses sell <u>very specialist</u> products that not many people want to buy. There probably won't be much competition as the market won't be big enough for many businesses to <u>survive</u>. For example, not many people have <u>houses</u> with <u>thatched roofs</u>. So there aren't many <u>qualified thatchers</u>, and the competition between them is <u>low</u>.

3) Some markets are <u>hard</u> to start a business in because the <u>cost</u> of setting up a new business is <u>too high</u>. This could be because the <u>equipment</u> needed is <u>expensive</u>, or because the employees require <u>specialist skills</u> meaning they may need lots of <u>training</u> and expect <u>high wages</u>. Not many businesses will be set up to sell to these markets, and there'll be <u>low</u> competition.

> 1) There's <u>very little competition</u> in the <u>commercial planes</u> market — Boeing and Airbus are the two main competitors.
>
> 2) It would be very <u>difficult</u> for a new company to start making planes. They'd need lots of <u>space</u> and the <u>equipment</u> and <u>materials</u> needed to build a plane would <u>cost a lot</u>. Employees also need to be <u>carefully trained</u> to make sure the plane is built <u>safely</u>.

BUSINESS EXAMPLE

I'm not competitive — I just really don't like losing...

PRACTICE QUESTION

Q1 State and explain the level of competition you think the following businesses will face:
   a) A shop selling clothes on a local high street.
   b) A company that specialises in reptile grooming.
   c) A pharmaceutical company selling a new, improved treatment for hay fever.

Globalisation

You might need your <u>passport</u> for this page — globalisation is all about businesses working around the <u>world</u>.

Globalisation Means the World is More Interconnected

1) <u>Globalisation</u> is the process by which businesses and countries around the world become more <u>connected</u>. It has resulted in single businesses operating in <u>lots of countries</u>. They can be <u>based</u> anywhere, and can <u>buy</u> from and <u>sell</u> to any country.

2) Globalisation means there's a much <u>larger market</u> that UK businesses can trade with — they're trading with people <u>all over the world</u>, not just people in their own town or country.

3) However, having a <u>global</u> market means there can be lots <u>more competition</u>. So UK businesses need to be able to <u>stand out</u> from the competition. Here are a couple of ways they do that:

- Many UK companies invest lots of money in <u>design</u>. This means they can <u>compete</u> in a global market by designing <u>new products</u> or <u>processes</u>.
- The UK has a <u>reputation</u> for producing <u>higher quality</u> goods and services than many other countries. By <u>maintaining quality standards</u> and taking measures to keep <u>prices lower</u> than overseas competitors (e.g. by being more efficient and taking advantage of economies of scale — see p.14), UK companies can <u>compete strongly</u> in a global market.

Globalisation can be a Good Thing for UK Businesses

1) Having a <u>larger market</u> to <u>sell to</u> can lead to <u>increased sales</u> and <u>higher profits</u>. Having a larger market to <u>buy from</u> means firms may be able to buy supplies <u>more cheaply</u>, which <u>reduces costs</u> and can lead to <u>higher profits</u>.

2) Globalisation means that it's easier for UK businesses to set up factories in other countries. This can reduce their <u>transport costs</u> if it means they're producing goods <u>closer</u> to certain parts of their market or closer to where <u>raw materials</u> are produced. It can also mean companies don't have to pay <u>import taxes</u> in the countries where they have factories.

3) Some companies will purposely set up factories in countries where <u>labour</u> is <u>cheaper</u>, which helps to keep their <u>costs down</u> and can increase their <u>profits</u>.

Globalisation has Drawbacks for UK Businesses

1) <u>Higher wages</u> in the UK means some UK industries <u>can't compete</u> with firms from other countries. E.g. <u>steel</u> from <u>China</u> is much cheaper than from the UK, partly because the average <u>wage</u> in China is <u>lower</u> than in the UK. So some UK industries such as <u>steel manufacture</u> have suffered from globalisation.

2) Other countries have <u>different currencies</u> to the UK. So if a business is <u>buying or selling</u> products in other countries, its profits are likely to be affected by changes in the <u>exchange rate</u> (see next page).

3) UK businesses that set up factories abroad to benefit from cheaper labour costs may get <u>bad publicity</u> if they're seen to be <u>exploiting</u> or <u>endangering</u> workers in these countries.

BUSINESS EXAMPLE

1) In 2012, a <u>fire</u> in a clothes factory in Bangladesh killed at least 117 people and injured over 200.

2) Many workers were <u>unable to escape</u>, partly because there weren't enough <u>emergency exits</u>.

3) <u>UK businesses</u> who outsourced their <u>clothing manufacture</u> to factories in Bangladesh came under scrutiny to make sure the factories they were using had a good level of <u>fire safety</u> and to <u>give money</u> to these factories to help them to improve their <u>working conditions</u>.

It's a small world after all...

Globalisation has been around for ages — the spice trade is an early example. But in the last century, better technology has meant that globalisation has become a much more important factor for businesses.

Exchange Rates

Exchange rates tell you how <u>currencies</u> compare. They're not only important for businesses — if you go <u>on holiday</u> to another country, exchange rates will determine how <u>expensive</u> it is to buy other currencies.

Exchange Rates Convert between Currencies

1) If a company wants to <u>import</u> products, they'll have to pay for the product in the <u>currency</u> of the <u>country</u> it was made in. For example, if a British firm is importing goods from the US, they'll have to pay for them in <u>dollars</u>, rather than <u>pounds</u>.

2) An exchange rate is the <u>price</u> at which <u>one currency</u> can be <u>traded for another</u>.

3) Exchange rates are affected by the <u>economy</u> of the country that uses the currency, and by the <u>global economy</u>. This means they can <u>change</u> over time.

> *Importing means buying goods from another country. Exporting means selling goods to another country.*

- In June 2016, the UK voted to leave the <u>European Union</u>.
- This created a lot of <u>uncertainty</u> about what would happen to the UK economy.
- As a result, the <u>value</u> of the <u>pound</u> dropped overnight.
- The day before the result was announced, £1 was worth $1.48. After the result was announced, £1 was worth just $1.36.

A Weak Pound is Good for Exporters, Bad for Importers

1) If the value of the pound <u>decreases</u>, you'll be able to <u>buy fewer dollars</u> (or other currency) for the <u>same price</u> as before.

2) Pounds are <u>cheaper</u>, so British <u>exports</u> become <u>less expensive abroad</u> — resulting in <u>more sales</u> and higher profits for British firms that export products to other countries.

3) The <u>weak pound</u> also makes it <u>more expensive</u> for <u>foreign firms</u> <u>to sell their products</u> in the UK. That's <u>good news</u> for British firms that compete with goods imported from abroad — they <u>won't</u> have to <u>reduce their prices</u> so much to stay competitive.

4) But it's <u>bad news</u> for <u>British firms</u> that use <u>imported raw</u> <u>materials</u> — these are now <u>more expensive</u> so the production costs of these firms are higher. They'll need to <u>increase</u> the price they <u>sell</u> their products for to cover their costs, which could cause their <u>sales</u> and <u>profits</u> to go down.

5) The result is that the UK will have <u>more exports</u> and <u>fewer imports</u>.

- If £1 = $1.50, a British cricket ball that costs £5 will sell in the US for 5 × 1.50 = <u>$7.50</u>. And a baseball that cost $6 in the US can be sold for 6 ÷ 1.50 = <u>£4</u> in the UK.

- If the value of the pound falls so that £1 = $1.30 the £5 cricket ball would sell in the US for 5 × 1.30 = <u>$6.50</u>. The $6 baseball can now be sold in the UK for 6 ÷ 1.30 = <u>£4.62</u>.

> *You don't need to be able to do these calculations — but make sure you understand how changing the exchange rate can affect the cost of importing or exporting.*

A Strong Pound is Bad for Exporters, Good for Importers

1) An <u>increase</u> in the value of the pound makes <u>exports more expensive</u> and <u>imports cheaper</u>. It's just the <u>opposite effect</u> to the example above.

2) British firms that <u>export</u> products to other countries are likely to see their <u>sales</u> and <u>profits go down</u> — their products will be <u>more expensive</u> so fewer people will buy them.

3) British firms that <u>import</u> raw materials will be able to make products <u>more cheaply</u>, so their profits may <u>go up</u>.

---

1 sultana = 0.84 raisins on the currant exchange...

This is a difficult page, so check you really understand it all. A weak pound means it's expensive to buy things from abroad, and cheap for people from abroad to buy things from us. A strong pound means the opposite.

Risks in Business

Hold on to your hard hats and grab your high-vis jackets — running a business can be a risky thing...

Different People Start Businesses for Different Reasons

Here are some possible reasons why people might want to start a business...

1) Lots of entrepreneurs have the financial objective of becoming rich from their share of the profits made by their business.

2) Some entrepreneurs have non-financial objectives, like the freedom of being their own boss, following an interest or to leave a job they don't enjoy.

3) For many people, running a business is a challenge that they enjoy.

4) Some people start a business because they want to benefit others. This could be done by starting a charity, or by having social objectives for their business.

There's more about entrepreneurs and why they start businesses on page 3.

There are Lots of Risks in Running a Business

All businesses face risks and uncertainties — whether they're new or established, big or small. For example:

1) STARTING A BUSINESS. To start a business, an entrepreneur needs money to buy equipment and pay workers. An entrepreneur will often use their own money, but they'll probably need to raise more from banks or other investors as well. If the business doesn't make enough profit to pay back all the money that's been borrowed, it will fail and lots of the money that's been invested in the firm will be lost.

2) THE HEALTH OF THE ECONOMY. This can affect all sorts of things — including unemployment levels, interest rates and exchange rates. If these things change, they can have a big impact on a business. For example, it can affect the demand for products and how much investment there is in the business.

3) THE ACTIONS OF COMPETITORS. Few firms know exactly what their competitors are planning. If a competitor brings out a new product or claims more market share then a firm may struggle to survive.

Businesses can do Certain Things to Reduce the Risks

Nobody wants their business to fail. Luckily, there are a few things that business owners can do to help make sure that their business is a success.

There's no way our plan for global domination can fail. All the planning has been top notch.

Planning

1) Doing a proper business plan (p.12) at the start makes a new business less likely to fail.

2) Established businesses also need to make plans in order to change or grow the business.

3) However, things don't always go to plan. Businesses need to have 'plan Bs' in place to prepare for different scenarios. E.g. if a business's main supplier suddenly goes bust, the business should already have the details of other suppliers that they can use.

Researching

1) Businesses should carry out regular market research to make sure they've got the right marketing mix for their products (p.53) — this means they should be selling the right products to people who want to buy them in a place where these people will be, and at the right price.

2) Businesses should research their competition. This means they will be more aware of any new competitors and can keep up with any new products or pricing that competitors have brought in.

3) Businesses need to make sure they're aware of any planned changes to the law or predicted changes to the economy that could affect them. This allows them to prepare for the changes and make sure they have the best plans in place for dealing with them.

Be careful of the baking industry — it's full of whisks...

Running a business is risky. Regular planning and researching are crucial if a firm is going to survive long-term.

Case Study — Influences on Business

Time to see how much this section has influenced your brain, with a good old case study.
Read through the information carefully, and then have a go at the questions that follow.

Business Report: Influences on Business

Aldi

The supermarket chain Aldi sells mainly own-brand products at cheaper prices than many other UK supermarkets. Aldi has a number of social and environmental policies. For example, it aims to pay staff in the UK above the National Minimum Wage (or National Living Wage for people aged 25 and over). This meant that in February 2016, people in entry-level jobs were paid at least £8.40 per hour. Many of the goods in Aldi's UK stores are also British. For example, all the fresh meat in UK stores comes from Britain. It also has a policy not to send waste from its stores to landfill.

Between 2008 and 2014, Aldi's market share increased. The graph on the right shows how the average disposable income of a household changed during this time. (Disposable income is the money that remains after taxes have been taken off a person's income.)

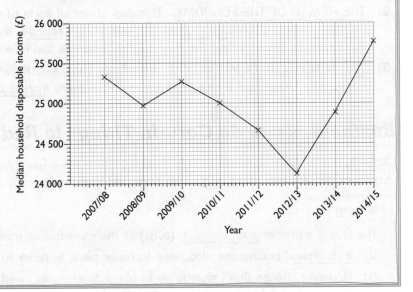

Case Study Questions

All that information wasn't just so you can ace a general knowledge quiz.
You'll need to use it to answer the following questions.

1) Explain two things that Aldi are doing that may give them a competitive advantage.

2) Using the graph, suggest an explanation for why the market share of Aldi changed as it did.

3) Describe and explain how Aldi's UK profits may have been affected by the following factors:
   a) The introduction of the National Living Wage at £7.20 per hour in April 2016.
   b) The fall in the value of the pound in June 2016.

Aldi information is giving me a headache...

Case studies may not be the most fun thing in the world, but it's important to practise answering questions like these before the exams. Remember — you already have the knowledge. The key is to apply it to a new situation.

Revision Summary

Things are always changing in business. Business owners have to stay aware of all the influences covered in this section if they want their business to have a chance of surviving. And in the exams, you need to be aware of them too. So have a go at these questions to test how much you remember.

1) Describe the difference between people who are entitled to the National Minimum Wage and people who are entitled to the National Living Wage.
2) Briefly describe what the Equality Act 2010 states about recruitment in a business.
3) How might a business be affected if it fails to obey the Equality Act 2010?
4) True or false? Businesses are legally obliged to provide employees with necessary safety equipment.
5) State two possible consequences to a business of failing to follow the Health and Safety at Work Act 1974.
6) State three criteria that goods should meet in order to follow consumer law.
7) Explain why breaking consumer law can be expensive for a business.
8) How does e-commerce affect the market a business can sell to?
9) Briefly describe how businesses can use social media to communicate with customers.
10) Other than social media, state three ways a business can communicate digitally with its stakeholders.
11) Describe three ways in which a firm could make sure it is working ethically.
12) Explain why working ethically might reduce a firm's profits.
13) State two ways in which a business could reduce the damage it causes to the local environment.
14) What does it mean if a business is trying to become more sustainable?
15) Explain one way in which a business could reduce its impact on global warming.
16) State two negative impacts that high levels of unemployment can have on a business.
17) Describe a type of business that could suffer if prices are rising at a faster rate than incomes.
18) Explain what happens to consumer spending when interest rates fall.
19) Explain how a firm with lots of loans will be affected by rising interest rates.
20) Describe three meanings of the term 'market'.
21) Describe what is meant by the term 'competitive market'.
22) Describe two ways being in a competitive market can affect a business.
23) State one reason a business might not face much competition.
24) What is globalisation?
25) Explain two ways in which a UK business might benefit from globalisation.
26) Explain two ways in which globalisation might have a negative effect on a UK business.
27) What is an exchange rate?
28) Explain why a weak pound can benefit companies that export goods.
29) Explain how a strong pound can affect a business that imports goods.
30) State two reasons why people start businesses.
31) Give two uncertainties faced by all businesses.
32) Describe two things a business can do to minimise the risks of failing.

Supply Chains

Business operations are the <u>activities</u> needed for the business's <u>day-to-day functioning</u>. There's quite a lot of different things that businesses have to <u>juggle</u> to get their operations <u>just right</u>. First up, <u>supply chains</u>...

Businesses Need to Have Dependable Supply Chains

1) A <u>supply chain</u> consists of the <u>group</u> of firms that are involved in <u>all</u> the various <u>processes</u> required to make a <u>finished product</u> or <u>service</u> available to the customer.

2) The chain <u>begins</u> with the <u>provider of raw materials</u> (supplier) and <u>ends</u> with the firm that sells the <u>finished product</u>.

3) The members of a supply chain will <u>vary</u> depending on the type of product or service, but will typically include <u>suppliers</u>, <u>manufacturers</u> (firms that make products) <u>distributors</u> and <u>retailers</u>.

4) <u>All</u> the <u>members</u> of the supply chain need to be <u>dependable</u>. If any are <u>unreliable</u>, the product won't be on the shelves when it needs to be, or the <u>quality</u> will be <u>poor</u>, which reflects <u>badly</u> on the company selling it.

A distributor usually buys products from a manufacturer and sells them on to other businesses or consumers (people like me and you). A retailer sells products directly to consumers.

Companies Need to Choose Their Suppliers Carefully

Often there are <u>many different firms</u> that could <u>supply</u> a business with what they need. There are some <u>important factors</u> to consider when <u>choosing</u> which supplier to use:

1 — Price (the total cost of getting the product)

- Firms have to decide <u>how much</u> they are willing to <u>pay</u> and whether cost is their <u>first priority</u>.
- If they want to <u>cut down</u> the <u>time</u> it takes to serve customers, suppliers that offer <u>faster delivery</u> may <u>rate higher</u> than those that compete on price alone.
- Also, <u>cheaper</u> suppliers will often supply <u>lower quality</u> products. The firm needs to <u>balance reduced costs</u> with the <u>quality</u> of the <u>product or service</u> it wants to provide.

2 — Quality

- The quality of supplies needs to be <u>consistent</u>.
- The growth of the <u>internet</u> means that customers can be much more <u>selective</u> about <u>quality</u> — it's easier for them to <u>shop elsewhere</u> if they're not happy with the quality of a product.
- <u>Customers</u> will associate poor quality with the business they <u>buy</u> from, <u>not</u> their <u>suppliers</u>.

3 — Reliability

- If a <u>supplier</u> lets a firm down, that firm may not be able to <u>supply</u> its <u>own customers</u>.
- Suppliers need to deliver <u>high-quality</u> products <u>on time</u>, or give plenty of warning if they can't.

1) <u>KI Holdings Co Ltd.</u> make passenger <u>seats</u> for <u>aeroplanes</u>.
2) They had a <u>contract</u> to supply <u>Thai Airways International Public Company Ltd.</u> with economy seats for its aeroplanes.
3) However, it was <u>late</u> delivering some of these seats and <u>failed to deliver</u> some of the seats at all.
4) This meant that Thai Airways had to <u>find another seat supplier</u>. This process took around <u>18 months</u>, during which time Thai Airways <u>couldn't use</u> five aeroplanes that needed seats.

BUSINESS EXAMPLE

Chinese, Indian, kebab shop — I love choosing my supplier...

Suppliers are really important in any supply chain. If they're late or supply shoddy goods then it can have serious knock-on effects further down the chain. Bosses need to wear their 'serious business' hats when choosing suppliers.

More on Supply Chains

A <u>supply chain</u> needs to be <u>well-managed</u>, but that isn't always easy peasy lemon squeezy. It involves <u>buying</u> the right goods or services and making sure things are <u>where</u> they need to be <u>when</u> they need to be there.

Procurement and Logistics are Really Important in a Business

1) <u>Procurement</u> means <u>finding</u> and <u>buying</u> things that a firm needs from suppliers <u>outside</u> of the firm. E.g. for a clothes manufacturer, procurement would involve <u>finding</u> and <u>buying</u> the material it needs.

2) <u>Logistics</u> means getting <u>goods</u> or <u>services</u> from <u>one part</u> of the supply chain <u>to another</u>. E.g. a clothes manufacturer would need to have the material it needs <u>transported</u> to its factory.

3) Having effective procurement and logistics systems in place <u>improves</u> the <u>efficiency</u> of a business — the business will have the supplies it <u>needs</u> at the <u>right time</u>. This means, for example, there will be <u>no breaks in production</u> because materials aren't available, or that materials don't have to be <u>wasted</u> because they arrived too early or weren't really needed.

4) Effective procurement and logistics can reduce the <u>overall costs</u> of a business. If a business gets its supplies at the <u>best price</u> and it doesn't <u>waste money</u> by being <u>inefficient</u> it will have lower overall costs. This will <u>reduce</u> the <u>unit cost</u> — the amount it <u>costs</u> to make <u>each item</u>. So the firm can make <u>more profit</u> on each item or pass the savings on to the consumer by <u>reducing prices</u>.

Managing a Supply Chain Effectively is Very Important

Companies that <u>manage</u> their <u>supply chain effectively</u> gain these <u>benefits</u>:

1 — Good Relationship with Suppliers

A company that <u>works closely</u> with its suppliers can make sure that processes are being carried out in ways that are most <u>efficient</u> and <u>cost-effective</u>.

2 — Finding the Best Price and Value

1) There are often <u>many suppliers</u> for a business to choose from.

2) Businesses that <u>research</u> potential suppliers can make sure they are getting the best <u>price</u> and <u>value</u> for the goods they need.

3 — Reducing Waste and Unnecessary Costs

1) Companies should <u>reduce waste</u> wherever they can. For example, they should only buy supplies they <u>really need</u>. This <u>reduces waste</u> from having to get rid of supplies that they <u>haven't used</u>.

2) Companies should reduce any <u>unnecessary costs</u> in their supply chain. For example, if their delivery trucks are only ever <u>half full</u>, it might be better to <u>get smaller</u> vehicles that are <u>cheaper</u> to run.

3) Reducing waste and unnecessary costs can help to make a business more <u>streamlined</u> (more efficient) and have <u>faster production times</u> — they have the supplies they need when they need them, and spend less time dealing with waste and other things that aren't really needed.

Spending all day buying stuff? Procurement sounds great...

Q1 A UK candle manufacturer gets its wicks from abroad. However, in recent years they have received several damaged batches of wicks that they couldn't use.

    a) In terms of logistics, suggest why it might be more efficient for the firm to use a UK supplier.

    b) The business has decided to negotiate a new arrangement with its current supplier. Explain one way in which managing its current supply chain more effectively may benefit the business.

Methods of Production

Once a business has got all the materials it needs, the products are <u>made</u> — this is called <u>production</u> or <u>manufacturing</u>. You need to know about <u>job production</u> and <u>flow production</u>.

Job Production is Making One Thing at a Time

1) Job production is used when a firm manufactures <u>individual</u>, <u>unique</u> products. Each product has a <u>unique design</u> based upon the <u>customer's specification</u>. If they're made in a factory, the firm will need to <u>retool</u> (install new equipment in) its factory each time it makes a new product.

As workers are highly skilled they're likely to be better paid than workers who make products by flow production (see below). This means job production workers may have more job satisfaction and be more motivated.

2) These products often require highly <u>skilled labour</u> and have a high <u>labour-to-capital ratio</u> (i.e. lots of workers are needed, but relatively little financial investment) — they can be very <u>labour-intensive</u>.

3) They're usually <u>expensive</u> and take a <u>long time</u> to make. But they're also <u>high quality</u>.

4) Examples include the building of <u>ships</u> and <u>bridges</u>, and handmade crafts such as <u>furniture making</u> and <u>made-to-measure</u> clothes.

Flow Production is Making Lots of Things Continuously

1) This is the <u>opposite</u> of job production. All products are <u>identical</u> and the aim is to produce as <u>many as possible</u> along an <u>assembly line</u>. To be efficient, production has to be <u>continuous</u> with no stoppages — many flow production factories operate 24 hours a day with workers rotating in <u>shifts</u>.

2) The aim is to gain from <u>economies of scale</u> (see p.14) and so have a low <u>average unit cost</u> (see p.11) to allow <u>competitive</u> prices. Modern flow production techniques use <u>robots</u>, not people, to do most of the work. Where workers do have jobs along the assembly line they are <u>simpler tasks</u> than in job production. Flow production is highly <u>capital-intensive</u> (it needs a lot of money — to buy machinery, for example) and may also require a lot of <u>space</u> for product <u>storage</u>.

Shouldn't have had that last cup of tea.

3) It is used for <u>mass-market</u> products. Most modern consumer goods are produced this way — <u>chocolate bars</u>, <u>mobile phones</u>, <u>televisions</u>... and so on.

Flow production is also sometimes called mass production.

Job production — it'd solve the unemployment crisis...

Q1 Which Stitch is a firm that makes costumes. In a recent pantomime production, Which Stitch were asked to make costumes for the five leading characters. The theatre company told the design team how they wanted each costume to look and each item was made to their unique requirements. The remaining cast's costumes were bought from a wholesaler (a firm that sells costumes in bulk at low cost).
a) What method of production does Which Stitch use?
b) Suggest two reasons why the theatre company didn't use Which Stitch for all of its costumes.

Production Efficiency

In efficient firms there's <u>no messing about</u> when it comes to production — they get products <u>made</u> and <u>out of the door</u> as <u>efficiently</u> as they can. <u>How many</u> supplies they need to do this and <u>when</u> they need them depends on the <u>strategies</u> used to <u>produce goods</u> and <u>store stock</u>.

Lean Production Increases Efficiency of Production

1) Lean production is a <u>strategy</u> businesses can use to make production <u>more efficient</u>.

2) In lean production, the business aims to use as <u>few resources</u> as possible and to have as <u>little waste</u> as possible.

3) <u>Workers</u> can also be encouraged to <u>think about ways</u> to improve their <u>productivity</u> (how much they can produce in a given time).

Products can be Made 'Just-in-Time'

1) <u>Just-in-time</u> (<u>JIT</u>) is a form of <u>lean production</u>.

2) JIT aims to keep <u>stock levels</u> to the bare <u>minimum</u> — preferably zero.

3) Ideally, all <u>raw materials</u> come in one door, are made into <u>products</u> and go <u>straight out</u> another door — all '<u>just in time</u>' for delivery to customers.

4) <u>Computer systems</u> are usually used to <u>calculate stock levels</u> and <u>automatically</u> order more when more supplies are needed.

The Way Stock is Managed can Also Affect a Firm's Efficiency

<u>Managing stock</u> is really important for a business — the <u>more they have</u> the more it <u>costs</u> to store, but if they have <u>too little</u> then they risk <u>running out</u>. There are <u>two</u> methods used to manage stock that you need to know about:

Just-in-Time (JIT)

- As well as being a type of <u>lean production</u>, JIT is also a way of <u>managing stock</u>.

- The main <u>benefit</u> of JIT is that it <u>reduces</u> the <u>cost</u> of having to <u>keep stock</u> (you need less warehouse space, fewer warehouse workers, and so on).

- The main <u>problem</u> is that it requires a lot of <u>coordination</u> between the firm and its suppliers. The firm needs to take lots of <u>frequent deliveries</u> of stock — this will be more <u>costly</u> for the firm. Also, if any of these deliveries don't arrive <u>on time</u> or there are <u>mistakes</u> with the order, the firm could <u>run out of stock</u>.

- A JIT method also means that firms buy <u>small quantities</u> of stock at a time, rather than buying in <u>bulk</u>. This means they <u>lose out</u> on <u>purchasing economies of scale</u> (see page 14).

Just-in-Case (JIC)

- JIC is a method of operating a production and distribution system with <u>buffer stocks</u> (extra stocks) of items at every stage of the process — from raw materials to finished products — <u>just in case</u> there is a <u>supply shortage</u> or <u>customer demand increases</u> unexpectedly.

- The idea is that even if there's a problem with deliveries of any raw materials, the buffer stocks will mean there is still enough to <u>satisfy demand</u> so production can <u>continue</u>.

- The main <u>problem</u> is that firms can be left with big stockpiles of items, which can be <u>costly</u> to store.

'Just-in-time' is not the best approach when it comes to revision...

The word 'lean' means there's not much of something, which is how lean production gets its name. It's all about making quality products with as little as possible. Having no back-up can be mega stressful for the workers though.

Quality

Even the most productive business in the world won't get far if its products aren't up to scratch.

Customers Expect Quality from All Parts of a Business

1) Products should be good quality, of course. The quality can depend on different factors such as the materials the product is made from and the production method used to assemble the product (see p.34). At the very least, customers expect products to work properly, and not fall apart straight away.

2) For businesses that provide a service, the service needs to be good quality. For example, a bus company needs to make sure its buses are clean, well-maintained and arrive when they're supposed to.

3) Customer service (any interaction a business has with its customers) also needs to be good. Customers expect a high standard of service — businesses that deliver this usually do better than those that don't.

See pages 38-39 for more on customer service.

There Are Benefits and Costs Involved in Maintaining Quality

Benefits

1) HIGHER PRICE — Customers are often prepared to pay a higher price for better quality products — as long as they're still good value for money.

2) INCREASED SALES — When customers are pleased with the quality a business provides, they're likely to make repeat purchases (buy from the business again). This increases the business's sales.

3) BETTER REPUTATION AND IMAGE — Businesses that provide higher quality products are likely to have a better reputation and image than those that don't. This means new customers are more likely to choose them and existing customers will be encouraged to use them again.

Costs

1) STAFF TRAINING — To produce quality products, staff need to be doing their job properly — it's important that businesses spend money and time on training their staff well.

2) INSPECTION — Products need to be inspected to check the quality is good enough. The inspection process costs both time and money (see the next page for more).

Failing to Maintain Quality can Also Be Costly

1) DISRUPTED PROVISION OF SERVICES — if quality standards are not maintained, it may disrupt the services that a business can offer to its customers, meaning that it loses potential sales. E.g. if a cafe kitchen is found to be unhygienic, the cafe may close temporarily while it is cleaned.

2) PRODUCT RECALLS — Products need to be safe for the customer to use. If any product is found to be unsafe, products that have already been sold might have to be recalled (sent back to the manufacturer or distributor). The firms would have to offer the customers a refund or a replacement too. This can be very costly for the firms involved and can negatively affect their reputation and image.

BUSINESS EXAMPLE

1) In August 2016, Samsung launched its Galaxy Note7 smartphone.

2) After just weeks on the market, there were several reports of the phones overheating and in some cases catching fire.

3) As the products were thought to be unsafe, Samsung recalled 2.5 million of the phones.

4) Customers were offered a different phone or a refund, which was very costly for the firm.

Another quality tip from CGP...

You might not think you're particularly fussy about what you buy, but I bet you soon notice when quality falls below what you're expecting. Like when you get sticky notes that just fall off everything, or rubbers that just make big smudges on your page, or revision guides that don't have HILARIOUS jokes and pictures in.

Quality Management

Firms need to make sure they're maintaining quality standards, but this can get tricky as the firm grows.

Firms Need to Measure Quality

Before firms can determine whether their products are good quality, they need to clarify what good quality means to them and find ways to measure it. There are different ways a firm can measure quality. E.g.

- They can specify the physical properties of a product, e.g. its exact size, colour, ingredients, etc., and then test a random sample to check they meet these specifications (see below).
- They can monitor how many products get returned and how many customer complaints they get. The firm can decide what level of returns or complaints it is comfortable with.
- They can carry out customer surveys to assess how satisfied customers are with quality.

Quality Should be Regularly Checked During Production

1) Checking products as they're being made helps to identify quality problems before a product gets to the customer. Products are usually checked at three different stages of the production process.

STAGE 1	STAGE 2	STAGE 3
Check raw materials from suppliers.	Random samples taken to check quality of work in progress.	Random samples taken of finished products — items removed if they don't meet required quality.

2) Defects may be spotted before they have finished making the products, reducing waste.

3) The process can be expensive (sometimes whole batches of goods might need to be scrapped). But the cost to the business would be greater if dissatisfied customers returned their products or stopped buying their products.

Total Quality Management (TQM) — a Culture of Quality

1) The TQM strategy aims to make quality the responsibility of every employee in a firm, in order to make sure that quality remains consistent. Employees are encouraged to think about the needs of the customer. The focus is on getting things right first time — this reduces costs by cutting down on waste.

2) There is an emphasis on the quality of after-sales service as well as on the quality of production, both of which will increase customer satisfaction.

3) A downside of TQM is that it takes a long time to introduce. Workers need training so that they see quality as their responsibility — employees can get demotivated as it may seem like a lot of extra work.

Rapid Growth Makes it Hard to Maintain High Quality

Rapid growth ruined my life.

Waaah! Aaiee!

For businesses, growth is good — but success can bring its own problems. When a business starts to grow very quickly, its output of products will need to increase quickly too. Making sure quality standards stay high can become more difficult.

1) It may become expensive to carry out all the necessary quality inspections.

2) A business can also be overwhelmed by orders and cut corners to make products quicker.

3) One solution is to take on more employees — but it takes time to train new workers. Businesses have to be careful that standards don't fall in the meantime.

4) The business might become a franchisor (see p.15) — ensuring high quality standards are maintained across the franchises can involve a lot of staff training and regular inspections.

5) The business might outsource some tasks (pay another firm to do them). It can be expensive to outsource to a firm that delivers high quality (but using a cheaper firm can lead to a fall in quality).

TQM — my parents had that sussed when they created me...

PRACTICE QUESTION Q1 Partee Maxx is a business that organises events.
Outline two ways in which Partee Maxx could measure quality in their business.

Customer Service

All businesses <u>love</u> their customers. But like any relationship, things can get rocky from time to time. If you don't give your customers the right <u>service</u>, they might just lose their patience and dump you.

Customers Want Good Service Throughout the Sales Process

A <u>sales process</u> might involve these steps:

- <u>Finding</u> potential <u>new customers</u> — e.g. a company selling <u>jet skis</u> could have a <u>stand</u> at a <u>boat show</u>. They could ask people to leave <u>contact details</u> if they'd be <u>interested</u> in knowing more about jet skis.
- <u>Approaching</u> potential customers — e.g. <u>calling people</u> who left their contact details at the boat show and <u>inviting</u> them into the <u>showroom</u>.
- <u>Assessing</u> the customer's <u>needs</u> — e.g. finding out <u>what sort</u> of jet ski the person might want.
- <u>Presenting</u> — e.g. <u>showing</u> a customer a suitable jet ski in the showroom, <u>telling</u> them all about it and <u>persuading</u> them to <u>buy one</u>.
- <u>Closing</u> — e.g. getting the customer to <u>formally agree</u> to <u>buying</u> a jet ski (i.e. hand over their cash).
- <u>Follow-up</u> — e.g. <u>calling</u> the customer <u>after the sale</u> to check they are happy with their new jet ski.

Firms should provide <u>great customer service</u> throughout the <u>sales process</u>. Ways of doing this include:

1) Having Excellent Product Knowledge

1) Anyone in a firm involved in the <u>sales process</u> should know the firm's products <u>inside out</u>.

2) This is <u>important</u> for several reasons. For example:

   - Any <u>questions</u> customers have can be answered <u>quickly</u> and <u>accurately</u>.
   - Staff can make sure the customer is getting the product <u>most suited</u> to their needs, and may be able to sell them <u>additional products</u> to go with their initial purchase.
   - The customer feels more <u>confident</u> buying from the firm — if staff seem like they don't really know what they're talking about, the customer may be <u>wary</u> about buying from them.

2) Engaging Well with the Customer

1) Firms should ensure that any <u>experience</u> customers have with them is as <u>positive</u> as possible.

2) This involves staff being <u>polite</u> and <u>friendly</u> with customers and making them feel <u>important</u> and <u>valued</u>. Customers shouldn't feel like they're being <u>pushed</u> into making a purchase, nor should they feel like sales staff <u>aren't listening</u> to what they want in a product.

3) Firms often think of <u>extra ways</u> to make the experience for the customer <u>more positive</u>, such as offering <u>free refreshments</u> or <u>next-day delivery</u>.

3) Offering Post-Sales Service

Providing good customer service <u>doesn't end</u> when the sale is complete. The firm needs to be available for their customers <u>afterwards</u> as well.

- The firm may offer <u>user training</u> — teaching the customer how to use the product they've bought.
- Some businesses have a specific <u>after-sales helpline</u> — customers can <u>contact</u> this to help resolve <u>any issues</u> they have with the product, e.g. if it's <u>not working</u> as they expected.
- Some products, like cars and boilers, might need to be <u>serviced</u> throughout their lifespan — firms can often do this for their customers.

The tennis company failed — their service was broken...

Providing good customer service is really important. For example, a coffee shop might serve the best cup of coffee in the whole world, but if the staff all laugh at your hair and won't give you a clean spoon, you might not go back.

More on Customer Service

Advances in technology are just great — for one thing they've allowed firms to develop their customer service.

Customer Services are Developing via...

As the internet continues to grow and people can access it more and more easily (e.g. via tablets and smartphones), more customers are going online to buy products, find out information and communicate. This is changing the ways in which firms interact with their customers and so provide customer service.

1) Websites and E-commerce

Companies may buy and sell their goods online — this is called e-commerce (see pages 67-68) and can be done via a website. However, companies that provide a service also have websites. A website can be a really good way to provide good customer service, for example:

- Many firms include 24-hour ordering on their websites, so it's easier for customers to buy.
- Many sites provide answers to frequently asked questions (FAQs) so that customers can look up answers to queries. They also usually have contact details and provide online forms that customers can use to make enquiries or complain. Some even have a 'live chat' feature, so messages can be sent back and forth between a customer and an employee straight away.
- Some firms let customers set up online accounts so they can access services on the web (e.g. they can pay bills, top up their mobile phone credit, etc.).

2) Social Media

1) Social media includes websites (e.g. Facebook®, Twitter) and applications that allow people to communicate and share content online.

2) Firms can use these to communicate with customers, e.g. to show them how to use a product, or to let them know about offers or any changes to store opening hours.

3) It's also a quick and easy way for customers to contact a business, e.g. if they have a query or complaint. However, comments on social media may be seen by thousands of other people within minutes, so it's really important that businesses respond quickly and politely to any questions or complaints. This helps to give the firm a positive image, and is a good way to provide good customer service.

Providing Good Customer Service is Really Important

Benefits of Good Customer Service	Dangers of Poor Customer Service
1) Good customer service leads to high levels of customer satisfaction.	1) If a company provides poor customer service they're likely to have dissatisfied customers.
2) Satisfied customers are more likely to remain loyal to the company and make repeat purchases from them in the future.	2) People like to tell others about poor customer service they have received, so the tale of poor customer service may quickly spread by word of mouth (especially when social media is involved). The business ends up with a poor reputation and falling revenue.
3) Customers may be persuaded to spend more with a company that provides them with good customer service.	

Good customer service costs money — e.g. the wages of extra staff, and costs of providing after-sales care. For a small firm, these costs may be a major part of their spending. But customer service is crucial — most firms recognise that the benefits of customer service outweigh the costs, and ultimately increase profitability.

Not all customers need a good service — some just need a lie down...

Firms are certainly kept on their toes with all this new technology around. Customers are starting to expect more than just a snazzy website — for example, they like dependable, user-friendly apps and live chats too. Fussy things.

Case Study — Business Operations

Businesses have to work really hard keeping everything running smoothly so that customers are kept happy. See if you can apply what you've learnt to a real business example.

Business Report: Business Operations

Marks and Spencer

Marks and Spencer plc is a large retailer with around 900 stores in the UK and over 400 stores overseas. It is well-known for providing customers with high quality goods.

Marks and Spencer works closely with the factories that supply it with products. Each factory must meet minimum standards set by Marks and Spencer, otherwise they risk having their orders cancelled and no longer being used as a supplier. For example, one of the minimum standards is that each batch of products made in a factory must have a batch card. This card should detail all the processes that the product has been through in the factory and include the name of the worker that was in charge of each process.

Marks and Spencer has had instances in its history where mistakes have been made with quality management and products have had to be recalled. For example, in 2016, packs of tuna fishcakes were recalled as they contained egg, which was not stated on the label and could cause harm to someone with an egg allergy.

Marks and Spencer is constantly changing to keep its customers happy. In response to feedback from workers and customers, Marks and Spencer no longer plays music in its stores. It has a website that customers can use to buy their whole range of products, from flowers to furniture. The website also allows customers to track their orders online and has a live chat option if customers would like to speak to someone about a product. Marks and Spencer also has an official Facebook® page.

Case Study Questions

Think about what you have learnt about business operations to answer the following questions.

1) Describe one way Marks and Spencer effectively manages its supply chain and explain the benefit of this.
2) Explain how the use of batch cards is an example of a total quality management strategy.
3) Other than the direct financial costs, explain how the recall of tuna fishcakes may have negatively affected Marks and Spencer.
4) Analyse the ways in which Marks and Spencer provides good customer service, including how advances in technology have helped this to develop.

On your Marks (and Spencer's)...

... get learning. Business operations are important in any firm, so make sure you understand it all before exam time.

Revision Summary

In case you missed the title at the start, this section has been about Business Operations. Operations are the processes that make a business tick — if these processes break down, the whole business might grind to a halt.

1) What is a supply chain?
2) List four types of business that are usually part of a supply chain.
3) Give three important factors that a business should consider when choosing a supplier.
4) What does procurement mean?
5) What does logistics mean?
6) Explain how effective procurement and logistics can improve the efficiency of a business.
7) Explain how effective procurement and logistics can affect the unit cost of products.
8) Explain why a good relationship with suppliers is a benefit of managing a supply chain effectively.
9) Why is it important that a firm reduces waste and unnecessary costs in its supply chain?
10) a) What is meant by 'job production'?
    b) Give an example of a product made by job production.
11) a) What is meant by 'flow production'?
    b) Give an example of a product made by flow production.
12) Give one advantage of flow production over job production.
13) What does lean production mean?
14) What is meant by a just-in-time (JIT) production method?
15) Give one advantage of using JIT stock control.
16) Explain why a business may prefer to use a just-in-case (JIC) approach rather than JIT.
17) Give three reasons why it's good for a business to ensure customers get products that are good quality.
18) Give two costs associated with maintaining quality standards.
19) Why is it advantageous for a business to spot quality problems in the production process?
20) What does TQM stand for? And what does TQM involve?
21) Give one advantage of TQM.
22) Explain why each of the following may make it difficult for a growing business to maintain high quality standards:
    a) They become overwhelmed with customer orders.
    b) They franchise the business.
    c) They outsource some tasks.
23) Briefly describe the steps in a sales process.
24) Explain one reason why having good product knowledge allows sales staff to provide good customer service.
25) Give one way in which sales staff could make sure they engage positively with their customers.
26) Give three examples of post-sales services that a business might offer their customers.
27) Give three ways in which a business can help to make sure their website provides good customer service.
28) Explain how the growth in social media has allowed businesses to develop their customer service.
29) Explain why providing good customer service is important for customer loyalty.
30) Explain how poor customer service could lead to a big fall in a firm's revenue.

Internal Organisational Structures

Human resources is all to do with making sure a firm's employees are working as effectively as possible. There could be thousands of employees, so an internal organisational structure keeps track of how they're organised.

Organisational Structures Organise People

1) It's important that a firm has a clear internal organisational structure. This makes it easy for everybody in the business to know who is responsible for what, and helps the company to make sure that it has people in every job role to deal with each of its activities.

2) Most firms have a hierarchical structure — this means they are structured in layers.

3) There are four basic layers of staff within a hierarchy:

> *The number of people on each layer generally increases as you go down the hierarchy.*

- DIRECTORS are responsible for the business's strategy (its overall direction). The directors decide on strategy and targets at regular board meetings.

> *Managers and supervisors are responsible for planning, organising and decision-making.*

- MANAGERS organise the carrying out of the directors' strategy. A large firm may have senior, middle and junior managers.

- SUPERVISORS are ranked below managers. They usually look after specific projects or small teams of operatives.

- OPERATIVES are workers who aren't responsible for other staff. They're often given specific tasks to perform by managers or supervisors.

4) The directors are on the top layer of a hierarchy, and operatives on the lowest layer.

5) The chain connecting directors to operatives is called the chain of command.

6) At each level, a certain amount of responsibility is delegated (passed on) to people in the level below. The span of control is the number of workers who report to one manager in a hierarchy.

A Hierarchical Structure can be Tall or Flat

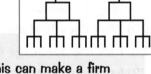

Tall Organisational Structures

- There is a long chain of command with more layers of management.
- In a tall structure each manager only has a narrow span of control. This can make a firm more effective as managers can monitor the employees they are responsible for more closely.

Flat Organisational Structures

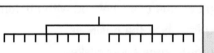

- There is a short chain of command.
- Each manager has a wide span of control. This means that each manager has to manage a lot of employees at once — it can be difficult to manage a lot of employees effectively.

1) The organisational structure that a business has can affect how the people within it communicate. It also depends on who is talking to who, and what they are talking about.

2) In a tall organisational structure, communication up and down the hierarchy can be difficult and slow as more people need to pass on the message. It can also be hard to use verbal communication (talking face-to-face or on the telephone) if lots of managers need to be involved in a conversation. Sometimes emails can be used to make communication faster, but they're not great when a discussion is needed, e.g. when making decisions. In this case meetings need to be set up in advance.

3) Communication up and down a flat organisational structure can be much faster because there are fewer layers of management. But verbal communication can still be tricky if a manager's span of control is very wide and they need to talk to each of their workers individually. However, if the manager needs to pass on the same message to each of their workers they can use emails or group meetings instead.

Sofa right in front of the TV — that's my internal organisation sorted...

A firm needs to have a balance between its span of control and chain of command. It's a tricky ol' business — if the span is too wide, or the chain is too long, communication within the business could start to suffer.

More on Internal Organisational Structures

Firms need to decide how much power to give to people at each layer of their organisational structures. E.g. too little power could make your minions unhappy, but too much and there could be chaos...

Organisations can be Centralised or Decentralised

How much power and authority is delegated at each layer in a hierarchy will depend on whether the bosses want a centralised or decentralised structure.

Centralised Organisations

1) All major decisions are made by one person or a few senior managers at the top of the hierarchy.

2) Advantages are that these senior managers tend to have plenty of experience, and can get an overview of the whole business. Policies will be uniform throughout the business.

3) On the downside, if all decisions need to be made by one or two people, it can slow down decision-making and communication of decisions can take a long time to filter through to employees. This means that the organisation reacts slowly to change.

4) Senior managers at the top of the hierarchy can become very powerful. But depending too heavily on a few people at the top can cause problems if those people lack specialist knowledge or if they 'lose their touch' and start making poor decisions.

Decentralised Organisations

1) The authority to make most decisions is shared out — for example, power might be delegated to regional managers or to more junior employees.

2) Advantages are that employees can use expert knowledge of their sector to make decisions. They don't always need to communicate these decisions with managers above them for approval, so changes can be made more quickly.

3) The disadvantages are that inconsistencies may develop between departments or regions. Also, the decision-makers might not be able to see the overall needs of the business.

1) Supermarket chains (e.g. Tesco, Asda) have a decentralised structure.

2) Big decisions on things such as branding and marketing campaigns are made by directors at the top of the hierarchy.

3) But each store usually has its own manager who makes important decisions about the running of their store, e.g. decisions about recruiting and training staff, and controlling stock levels.

BUSINESS EXAMPLE

Businesses Need to Choose the Most Appropriate Structure

1) The type of organisational structure a business has depends on many things, e.g. the business's size.

2) A small business is likely to have a flat structure — it's often just run by the owner without the need for any additional managers.

3) As the business grows and employs more staff, managers might be needed to help organise and control things, so the organisational structure gets taller.

4) The bigger the business, the greater the number of managers needed (and the greater the costs).

5) Over time, the business may delayer its structure to avoid becoming too tall — layers of management are removed (usually from the middle of the hierarchy). A business may also decentralise and encourage groups of workers to take more responsibility for their own self-management.

6) Businesses can also be organised into several areas — see next page for more.

Decentralisation — popular in the doughnut industry...

Firms often start with a centralised structure, but decentralise as they get too big to make all the decisions at the top. Understand the kind of effect that different structures can have on communication and you'll be doing great.

Other Internal Organisational Structures

As well as the authority of people within a business, the different <u>areas</u> of a business also need to be organised. For example, for proper <u>world domination</u> you need to have a N. America division, an Asia division etc. etc.

A Business Can be Organised by Function...

1) You get this a lot in <u>limited companies</u> (see p.6).

2) Each <u>functional area</u> does one part of the work of the business. Examples of functional areas are sales, marketing, customer service, operations, finance, human resources... and so on.

3) The main <u>advantage</u> is that <u>specialists</u> can concentrate on their particular job.

4) The main <u>disadvantage</u> is that the different departments may not <u>work well together</u>.

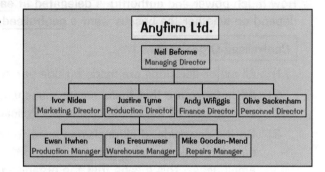

...Or By Product...

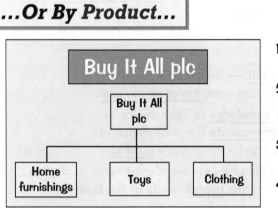

1) This is common with <u>large manufacturers</u> who make lots of different products.

2) A <u>product-based</u> structure splits the organisation into different <u>sectors</u>. For example, Buy-It-All PLC has three sectors — home furnishings, toys and clothing.

3) The main <u>advantage</u> is that managers can make decisions that are relevant to each product <u>sector</u>.

4) A <u>disadvantage</u> is that there can be a <u>wasteful duplication</u> of resources between sectors.

...Or By Region

1) This is normal for a <u>multinational</u> business.

2) The divisions may be <u>regional</u> or <u>national</u>.

3) The <u>main advantage</u> is that spreading management between regions makes <u>day-to-day control</u> easier.

4) A <u>disadvantage</u> is that there can be a <u>wasteful duplication</u> of resources between regions.

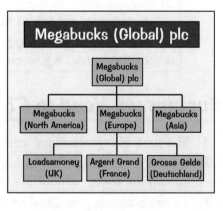

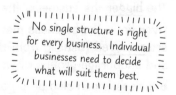

No single structure is right for every business. Individual businesses need to decide what will suit them best.

Organise by function — sort it out at a posh party...

Individual businesses have to find a structure that works for them — it's like really boring match-making...

Contracts of Employment

You need to know about different types of <u>contracts of employment</u>. To be more specific, you need to know about <u>part-time</u>, <u>full-time</u>, <u>job sharing</u> and <u>zero hour contracts</u>.

All Employees Have a Contract of Employment

A <u>contract of employment</u> is a <u>legal agreement</u> between an employee and an employer. It contains this information that most employers <u>must</u> give employees in writing within <u>two months</u> of starting work:

- the <u>job title</u> (or a brief job description)
- the <u>starting date</u> of the employment
- the <u>hours</u> of work, the <u>starting pay</u> and the regular <u>date of payment</u>
- <u>where</u> the employee will be working

- the <u>holiday</u> the employee's entitled to
- details of <u>sickness pay</u> and any <u>company pension</u>
- information about <u>disciplinary procedures</u>
- the length of <u>notice</u> the employee has to give if they want to leave

Employment Can be Full-Time or Part-Time

1) Working <u>full-time</u> usually means around <u>35-40 hours</u> a week.
   <u>Part-time</u> staff work 'less than a full working week' — <u>usually between 10 and 30 hours</u> per week.

2) Some people <u>prefer</u> to have a <u>full-time</u> job, or <u>need</u> to work full-time for financial reasons.
   Other people work <u>part-time</u> so they can spend more time with family or on other interests.

3) There are pros and cons for <u>businesses</u>. Full-time staff are good if there's enough work for them to do, since they are likely to have only one job and so the business will have more control over the hours they work. But employing staff <u>part-time</u> can make more <u>financial sense</u> if a business is only really busy at certain periods. Having part-time staff that can be <u>flexible</u> with their hours can also be good as they can fill in when other staff members are <u>absent</u> (e.g. due to sickness or holidays).

One Job Can be Shared Between Two People

1) Some employees <u>job share</u> — they share the <u>work</u> and <u>pay</u> of <u>one full-time job</u> with another person.

2) This is good for <u>employees</u> who only want to work <u>part-time</u> hours.

3) It can be good for <u>employers</u> because the two people might have <u>different strengths</u> that they bring to the job. It also means that if one person is <u>absent</u> (e.g. off sick), the other person might be able to work <u>extra hours</u> so the full job is still being done.

4) But for a job share to work, the <u>responsibilities</u> of each employee need to be very <u>clear</u> and the employees need to be able to <u>communicate</u> well with each other.

Zero Hour Contracts Allow Lots of Flexibility

Please, Rudolph!
It's just 8 hours.

Nope.

1) Some employees have <u>zero hour contracts</u> — this means that the employer <u>doesn't</u> have to offer them <u>any work</u> at all. Nor does the employee have to <u>accept</u> any work that is offered to them.

2) The contracts are used in businesses where there can be lots of <u>fluctuation</u> in demand, e.g. restaurants, hotels, care work.

3) They are a <u>cheap</u> form of labour for businesses — they don't <u>waste money</u> paying staff when they're not really needed and they don't need to pay <u>sick pay</u> or <u>holiday pay</u>.

4) Zero hour contracts might appeal to people who want to earn some <u>extra cash</u> but want to be able to <u>turn work down</u> if they're busy doing other things, e.g. students. But they can make it <u>hard</u> for people who <u>rely</u> on the work to <u>earn a living</u>.

I'm very flexible — one of those zero hour contracts will suit me fine...

Make sure you know the pros and cons of each type of employment and what's in a contract of employment.

Recruitment

Recruitment is the process of finding that special someone — that is, the best person to do a job. Businesses need to recruit people to increase their size, to gain new people with expertise or to replace staff that have left.

Businesses Need to Be Clear About the Job on Offer

There are several steps involved in recruitment — job analysis, advertisement and selection.

1) Job analysis is where a firm thinks in depth about every little detail of the job in question.

2) The business then advertises the job. This usually includes a job description and a person specification, which are produced from the job analysis.

- Job description — includes the formal title of the job, the main purpose of the job, the main duties plus any occasional duties. It will also state who the job holder will report to, and whether they will be responsible for any other staff.

- Person specification — lists the qualifications, experience, skills and attitudes needed for the job.

3) Then the business has to go through the candidates that apply and select the best one (see next page).

A Firm can Recruit People Internally or Externally

The purpose of a job advert is to get as many suitable people as possible to apply for the job.
Firms can use job adverts to recruit internally or externally:

Internally

- Internal recruitment involves recruiting current employees into new roles. The job position is advertised within the company.

- The advantages are that it's much cheaper, the post can be filled more quickly, the candidates will already know a lot about the firm, and bosses may already know the candidate well.

- On the downside, there will be no 'new blood' or new ideas, and the employee's move will leave a vacancy to fill.

Externally

- External recruitment involves recruiting from outside the business. The job can be advertised in lots of places, e.g. the local and national press, job centres, trade journals and employment websites.

- An advantage is that the job advert will be seen by more people, so it's more likely that the firm will find somebody really suited to the job.

- However, advertising externally isn't cheap — only specialist and senior jobs get advertised in the national press because it's very expensive.

It's Really Important That a Business Recruits the Right People

Getting the right people can have the following benefits for a business:

- High productivity — a person with the right skills and qualities for the job may only need minimal training and will be more productive than someone without these skills and qualities.

- High quality output — people with the best skills will make high quality products, e.g. if they already have experience making similar products.

- Good customer service — people well-suited to their role and who enjoy their job will provide better customer service.

- Staff retention — firms want to hold on to staff so that they don't have to keep recruiting people to replace them. If a person is recruited and finds out that the job isn't suited to them, they may leave.

> Staff retention is when a business keeps its staff.

Lonely business WLTM right person for ~~cuddles~~ hard graft...

PRACTICE QUESTION

Q1 A furniture manufacturer is recruiting sales staff for a new showroom. Following a job analysis, an advert for the role has been created and put up on noticeboards around the furniture factory.
  a) Describe what a job analysis is.
  b) Give two advantages of the firm advertising the role internally rather than externally.

More on Recruitment

Businesses usually like to have a <u>number</u> of candidates when they're trying to fill a vacancy.
The selection process then helps <u>compare</u> these candidates and decide which one is <u>best</u> for the job.

Candidates Explain Why They're Right for the Job

Businesses usually ask candidates to send a <u>written application</u> for a job.

1) A <u>curriculum vitae (CV)</u> is a summary of a person's personal details, skills, qualifications and interests. It's written in a <u>standard format</u> to give the firm the basic <u>facts</u>. Almost <u>all</u> firms ask for a CV.

2) Many businesses also ask candidates to fill in an <u>application form</u>. These forms give the firm the information it wants — and <u>nothing else</u>. This means they're much <u>quicker</u> to process and more <u>relevant</u> to the job than open-ended letters written by the candidates.

3) Many companies now like to use <u>online</u> application forms, where applicants fill in their details on the company's website. This allows the company to <u>compare</u> the applications using computer software.

<u>Shortlisted</u> candidates will usually be asked for <u>references</u>. These are statements about the character of the candidate written by someone who knows them — often a previous <u>line manager</u>.

References are usually <u>confidential</u> — the candidate won't see what's written about them.

An Interview is the Traditional Selection Method

1) Once the closing date for applications has passed, managers in the business make a <u>shortlist</u> of the best applicants. Shortlisted candidates are invited for an <u>interview</u> with at least one manager.

2) Interviewers should ask the <u>same questions</u> to <u>all candidates</u> so that the process is <u>fair</u>. They shouldn't ask questions that are <u>irrelevant</u> to the job or that unfairly <u>discriminate</u>.

3) Interviews are used to assess a candidate's <u>confidence</u>, their <u>social</u> and <u>verbal skills</u>, and whether they'll be <u>compatible</u> with existing workers. Businesses also want to find out about the candidate's general <u>attitude</u>.

Sorry. I can never behave naturally at interviews.

4) Some people think that interviews are <u>not a good way</u> to select — people don't behave <u>naturally</u> in a formal interview. The skills needed to be good at interview are often <u>different</u> from the skills needed to do the job.

Tests Can Also Help Select Who to Employ

1) Some businesses use <u>tests</u> — these are better than interviews for assessing the skills needed <u>for the job</u>. They can also be useful for spotting <u>differences</u> between <u>similar</u> candidates. There are four main types:

- <u>Skills tests</u> or <u>in-tray exercises</u> test whether the candidate has the <u>abilities</u> to do the job.
- <u>Aptitude tests</u> find out whether the candidate has the <u>potential</u> to learn how to do the job.
- <u>Personality tests</u> are used to assess the candidate's <u>personal qualities</u>.
- <u>Group tests</u> find out whether the candidate can work as part of a team — and whether they have good <u>leadership</u> and <u>decision-making skills</u>.

2) When all the candidates have been assessed, managers and **HR** staff meet to discuss how well the candidates have done. They then <u>select</u> the best candidates and offer them jobs.

Sick of recruitment methods? No need to get testy...

Businesses can often get hundreds of applications for one job. Reading application forms, conducting interviews and setting tests all take time — some businesses have a whole recruitment department to deal with this stuff.

Staff Training

Training is the main way that a firm invests in its employees. This page covers three basic types of training.

1) Induction Training is for New Staff

1) Induction training introduces the new employee to their workplace, and should help to make the new employee feel welcome.

2) It includes introducing them to their fellow workers and advising them of company rules and procedures. It may also include initial training on how to do their new job.

3) One advantage of induction training is that new employees feel confident when they start work. They are also less likely to make mistakes as they already know the basic procedures, meaning they can become productive as quickly as possible. They may also be more likely to stay in the job if they feel welcome and like a valued member of the team from the start.

2) On-the-Job Training is Learning by Doing

1) This is the most common form of training. The employee learns to do their job better by being shown how to do it, and then practising.

2) It's most suitable where practical skills are being taught, and when in a safe environment where communication is easy. For example, learning how to use a till in a shop or learning how to change a tyre in a mechanics workshop.

3) It's cost-effective for the employer because the employee works and learns at the same time.

4) A problem is that the training is often given by colleagues — so bad working practices can be passed on.

Yeah, we're supposed to lock the safe every night, but we never actually bother.

3) Off-the-Job Training is Not Done While Working

1) Off-the-job training happens when staff learn away from their workplace, e.g. at a local college.

2) Off-the-job training is appropriate when the employee needs to know general information about the business or procedures. It's useful for when employees are being trained for a promotion or are learning a new skill that isn't related to a specific task, e.g. learning how to touch type, or manage people.

3) It's more expensive than on-the-job training but it's often higher quality because it's taught by people who are better qualified to train others.

Training Benefits Both the Employer and the Employee

Benefits of training to EMPLOYERS

- Trained staff should be better at their jobs, which means they should be able to produce higher quality goods and provide better customer service. It should mean they're more efficient and productive too.
- Training can help staff stay up to date with changes in the business, such as knowing how to use new technology.
- Overall, training is likely to make staff feel motivated and like they're progressing in the firm. This might increase staff retention (see p.46) which will save on recruitment costs.

Benefits of training to EMPLOYEES

- Employees with up-to-date knowledge and skills should be able to do their jobs better, which often increases job satisfaction and motivation.
- Over time, gaining new skills may mean that they can be promoted to jobs with better pay and more responsibility.

'Bruno... Fetch me my slippers!' Sorry, just trying to train my Staffie...

Try to learn which types of training are best for different types of jobs. Go on, you know you want to...

Financial Motivation

Keeping staff <u>motivated</u> is important. Workers want to feel <u>valued</u> and that they're doing their jobs well. Firms can use <u>financial</u> methods (see below) or <u>non-financial</u> methods (see the next page) to keep staff motivated.

Motivated Staff are More Productive

1) Motivated staff can lead to <u>high productivity</u> — workers will want the business to do well and so will do their jobs as <u>well</u> as they can to help this happen.

2) Staff who are <u>motivated</u> and <u>happy</u> in their jobs are more likely to <u>stay</u> with the business. Having a high level of <u>staff retention</u> (see p.46) is good for a business as it means less <u>time</u> and <u>money</u> is spent having to recruit and train new workers.

Financial Motivation can be Wages or a Salary

1) Most people are <u>paid</u> for the <u>work</u> they do for an employer (some people might not be, e.g. if they're doing <u>voluntary</u> work).

2) Often, the <u>more</u> that a worker is paid, the <u>more motivated</u> they feel to do their job.

3) Workers can be paid with <u>wages</u> or with a <u>salary</u>.

4) <u>Wages</u> are commonly paid <u>weekly or monthly</u> — usually to <u>manual</u> workers. Wages are calculated in one of two ways:

> A <u>time rate</u> pays workers by the hour. It encourages people to work <u>long hours</u> — the problem is they also have an incentive to <u>work slowly</u>. Time rate is best for jobs where <u>measuring output</u> is <u>difficult</u> — like driving a bus.

> A <u>piece rate</u> is used if the <u>output</u> of each worker <u>can be easily measured</u> (such as a worker who sews sleeves onto shirts in a factory). Piece rates encourage people to <u>work quickly</u> — but if they work too fast, <u>quality may suffer</u>.

5) A <u>salary</u> is a <u>fixed</u> amount paid every <u>month</u> — this doesn't change even if the number of hours worked does change. It is usually paid to <u>office staff</u> who do not directly help to make the product. A salary of £24 000 means you are paid £2000 per month.

6) The advantage of a salary is that the firm and workers both <u>know exactly</u> how much the pay will be. However, it <u>doesn't</u> link pay directly to <u>performance</u>, so it doesn't encourage employees to <u>work harder</u>.

Employers can Give Staff Extra Payments

<u>On top</u> of their regular payments (wage or salary), some firms offer staff <u>extra financial incentives</u> to help to motivate them. For example:

1) <u>Commission</u> — this is paid to sales staff for <u>every item</u> they sell. It is given to them on top of a <u>small basic salary</u>.

2) <u>Profit sharing</u> schemes — for example, where a <u>percentage</u> of the company's <u>profits</u> is divided up between employees.

But I only wanted one...

BUSINESS EXAMPLE

- <u>John Lewis Partnership</u> is a business that employs around <u>90 000 permanent staff</u>.
- One of the main aims of the business is to keep its employees as <u>happy</u> and <u>motivated</u> as possible.
- Each year, John Lewis Partnership gives a <u>proportion</u> of its <u>profits</u> to its employees as a <u>bonus</u>. Each employee gets a <u>percentage</u> of their <u>salary</u>.

PRACTICE QUESTION

Financial rewards — I'm in it for the money, innit?

Q1 A hotel's rate of pay for a cleaner is higher than that of other local hotels. Explain how this might affect the productivity of the cleaners.

Non-Financial Motivation

When money alone won't do the trick, businesses have a few other tricks up their motivational sleeves...

Training Can Boost Motivation...

There's more on the benefits of training on page 48.

1) The main purpose of training is to help staff become better at their jobs.

2) But training can also improve motivation — being good at your job will boost your self-esteem.

3) Employees can also be trained to learn new skills. This means they can start to take on new tasks and have greater responsibility, which may stop them from becoming bored and make them more likely to want to stay with the firm.

4) They may even be told they could get a promotion once they have new skills, which may make them even more motivated.

...And Styles of Management Can Also Have an Effect

- Authoritarian (or autocratic) managers make decisions alone, without consulting staff.
- Paternalistic managers make decisions themselves, but only after consultation with workers.
- Democratic managers allow the workforce some influence over decisions.
- Laissez-faire managers allow workers to perform tasks as they see fit, offering help if needed.

1) Generally workers feel more motivated if they're managed in a way that lets them have some input into decision-making.

2) However, no single approach is perfect for all employees and all situations. E.g. the authoritarian style can demotivate staff if they feel their views aren't valued, but it can be effective when managing crises.

3) Often a mix of different management styles is used depending on the situation.

> **BUSINESS EXAMPLE**
>
> 1) Gillian is the head gardener at a large country estate. Her managers use a mix of different management styles.
>
> 2) Every year the estate has an open day for the public where they can look around the gardens. The managers consult Gillian while making plans for the open day, which makes her feel important and valued. This is an example of paternalistic management.
>
> 3) While Gillian is preparing the gardens for the open day the managers let her look after her own budget and solve problems on her own, which makes her feel trusted and engaged in her work. This is an example of laissez-faire management.
>
> 4) One year, a large area of the gardens flooded before the open day. The managers decided to fence off part of the gardens without consulting Gillian. Gillian was happy with this as she knew she didn't have the authority to make such big decisions. This is an example of authoritarian management.

Fringe Benefits are Extra Little Perks

This free gym membership is great. But what does the company get out of it?

1) A fringe benefit is any reward that is not part of a worker's main income.

2) Examples include staff discount on the firm's products, the use of a company car, gym membership, a daily meal allowance or free health insurance.

3) All of these perks cost money for the business, and save it for the worker — you could argue that they are a type of financial reward.

OFFICE POWER GENERATOR

The front of my hair gets extra conditioner — it's a fringe benefit...

Whether firms like it or not, employees are people too. They like to feel appreciated and be given responsibility in their jobs. And they probably won't complain if you pay for their lunch or give them a fancy car to drive either.

Case Study — Human Resources

Organising, recruiting, training and motivating people — there's a lot to remember in this section. It's time to apply what you've learnt about human resources to a case study.

Business Report: Human Resources

Lekker Lunch

Lekker Lunch is a rapidly expanding cafe chain. It has recently opened a new branch and recruited all of its ten floor and kitchen staff by advertising on the noticeboards at a local university. It has also recruited a supervisor for the new branch by promoting a member of the floor staff from another branch. The manager of the new branch also manages another two local Lekker Lunch branches. The organisational hierarchy of the business is shown on the right.

Lekker Lunch is employing half of its new floor and kitchen staff on zero hour contracts. The other staff are all employed on a part-time basis.

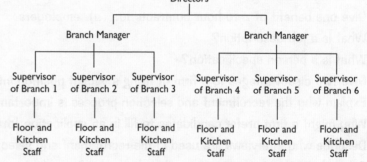

The new staff all received on-the-job training, which was given by the supervisor. The new staff were also given an information pack about Lekker Lunch. This included a brief description of the company and a staff discount card which entitled them to 30% off food at any Lekker Lunch cafe.

Case Study Questions

Think about what you've learnt about human resources to answer these questions.

1) Suggest one reason why Lekker Lunch advertised for its floor and kitchen staff on noticeboards rather than in the local or national press.

2) Suggest why Lekker Lunch chose not to employ any of its floor and kitchen staff on a full-time basis.

3) Give two reasons why a Lekker Lunch employee might be motivated to work for the company.

4) The supervisor in each branch has the authority to make certain decisions without consulting the branch manager. Explain one advantage and one disadvantage of this.

5) After three weeks, the supervisor reports that the new staff are still making lots of mistakes and some have said they are thinking of leaving as they don't feel confident doing their job. Explain why induction training might have been better than on-the-job training for the new staff.

It's nearly the end of Human Resources...

I don't mean we're all going to die. I mean you've just got a page of Revision Summary questions to go. Phew.

Revision Summary

Whoop-de-woo, the end of another section. And it wasn't too bad really — just a little bit of how people are organised and kept happy in a business. Here's something that might not keep you happy though — some revision summary questions to make sure you haven't been skim-reading too much...

1) What layer of staff is usually ranked immediately below directors?
2) What is meant by the span of control?
3) Which would have a longer chain of command — a company with a tall or a flat organisational structure?
4) How does the span of control differ between a tall and a flat organisational structure?
5) What is the difference between a centralised and a decentralised organisation?
6) Give one advantage of a centralised organisation.
7) Give two disadvantages of a decentralised organisation.
8) What is meant by the term 'delayering'?
9) Give three ways in which the different areas of a business might be organised.
10) What is a contract of employment? Give five things it should include.
11) What does it mean if a staff member is 'full-time'?
12) Give one advantage to an employer of having part-time staff.
13) What is job-sharing?
14) Give one benefit of zero hour contracts to: a) employers   b) employees.
15) What is a job description?
16) What is a person specification?
17) Give two disadvantages to a firm of filling a vacant position internally rather than externally.
18) Explain why the recruitment and selection process is important for customer service.
19) Why might a firm prefer candidates to fill in an application form rather than just send in their CV?
20) Describe why interviews are used in the recruitment and selection process.
21) Other than interviews, give one other method a firm might use to decide which shortlisted applicant to select for a job?
22) What is the purpose of induction training?
23) What is on-the-job training?
24) Explain what off-the-job training is and when it would be used.
25) Give one advantage of off-the-job training over on-the-job training.
26) Give two ways in which training benefits: a) employers   b) employees.
27) Explain how motivating staff affects staff retention in a business.
28) Explain two different ways in which an employee's wages may be calculated.
29) What does it mean if a business pays its employees commission?
30) Why might employees feel more motivated working for a democratic manager rather than an authoritarian manager?
31) What is meant by a 'fringe benefit'?
32) Give three examples of fringe benefits a firm might offer its employees.

The Marketing Mix

Human beings have <u>needs</u> — essential things like water, food and shelter. Once our needs are satisfied, we start to <u>want</u> luxuries too, and we're prepared to <u>pay</u> for them. <u>Marketing</u> is about coming up with a <u>product</u> that people need or want — then making it as <u>easy as possible</u> for them to buy it. Sounds simple enough...

There are Four Ps in Marketing

There are four <u>elements</u> to marketing: <u>product</u>, <u>price</u>, <u>promotion</u> and <u>place</u> — the four Ps. They're the <u>key</u> to understanding what marketing is all about. If a firm gets them <u>right</u> then customers will be more likely to <u>buy</u> its product. If it gets <u>even one</u> of them <u>wrong</u>, it's in <u>trouble</u> — <u>changing</u> one P may also have an <u>effect</u> on the <u>other Ps</u>. Together the four Ps are called the MARKETING MIX.

But I can't see any Ps in marketing...

1 — Product

The firm must first <u>identify</u> customers' needs (or wants). Then it needs to come up with a <u>product</u> that will <u>fulfil</u> some (or one) of these <u>needs</u>. So spinach flavoured sweets, for example, probably wouldn't sell that well.

Spinach sweets! Finally here to fulfil my every want and need!

2 — Price

The price must be one that the customer thinks is <u>good value</u> for money. This isn't the same as being <u>cheap</u>. You might be prepared to pay <u>a lot</u> of money for a <u>brand new</u>, 50-inch plasma-screen TV, but you'd expect an <u>old basic</u> 12-inch model to be much <u>cheaper</u>.

3 — Promotion

The product must be <u>promoted</u> so that potential customers are <u>aware</u> that it <u>exists</u>. It doesn't matter how good the product is — if no-one knows about it no-one will <u>buy</u> it.

4 — Place

It must be sold in a place that the customer will find <u>convenient</u>. That's why you can buy <u>buckets</u> and <u>spades</u> at the <u>beach</u>, <u>goggles</u> at <u>swimming pools</u>, and <u>petrol</u> at roadside <u>service stations</u> — they're the most convenient places for people to buy these products. <u>Place</u> can also refer to the <u>channel of distribution</u> (see p.66) used for a product. For example, whether it is sold through <u>retailers</u>, <u>wholesalers</u> or <u>straight</u> to a customer.

The Marketing Mix is Different for Different Products

1) Depending on the situation, some of the Ps might be <u>more important</u> than others.

2) For example, if customers <u>really want</u> the <u>product</u>, or it's in a <u>really convenient place</u>, they may be prepared to pay a <u>higher price</u>.

3) Alternatively, customers may be prepared to go to a <u>less convenient place</u>, or buy a product that isn't <u>exactly</u> what they <u>want</u>, if the <u>price is lower</u>.

4) Customers' needs and wants usually <u>change</u> over time — a business should <u>adapt</u> its marketing mix to <u>meet</u> these changing needs.

5) For example, customers used to buy music on <u>vinyl records</u> from a <u>shop</u>. Nowadays they're more likely to <u>download</u> music from the <u>internet</u>. The <u>product</u> and <u>place</u> have changed. So, many <u>record stores</u> now have <u>websites</u> where music can be downloaded.

Well, it's not the luxury model I had in mind, but it certainly is cheap...

You need to be able to say how well a business has adapted to changing needs over time, and also suggest what changes it should make to its marketing mix.

I want it all — and I want it now (in the right place at the right price, please)...

A good marketing mix makes customers want to spend money on your product. But customers' needs change — businesses need to be on their toes to make sure the marketing mix also changes to keep up.

Market Research

Market research involves <u>finding out</u> what customers want (what they really, really want)...

Different Markets Have Different Structures

1) You might remember from p.26 that a market can be a <u>meeting place</u>, trade in a particular <u>type of product</u> (e.g. the oil market), or a <u>group of people</u>.

2) Businesses often want to know about the <u>structure</u> of a market.

3) For example, it can be useful to know the <u>market size</u> and a business's <u>market share</u>.

4) The <u>market size</u> is the number of individuals (including companies) within the market which are <u>potential buyers</u> or <u>sellers</u> of products. It can also mean the <u>total value</u> of <u>products</u> in the market.

5) The <u>market share</u> of a business is the <u>proportion</u> of total sales within the market that is controlled by the <u>business</u>.

> Market research can help to identify the size of a market and the market shares of different businesses within that market.

Markets are Segmented into Different Groups of People

1) As well as understanding <u>market size</u> and <u>shares</u>, it can be useful to know how a market is <u>segmented</u>.

2) <u>Segmentation</u> is when <u>people</u> within a market are divided into different <u>groups</u>.

3) Knowing the different market segments can allow businesses to identify their <u>target market</u> — this is the specific group of people that a product is <u>aimed</u> at (see below).

4) They can then create a <u>marketing strategy</u> aimed at their target market (<u>a targeted marketing strategy</u>) to make sure that their marketing is as <u>effective</u> as possible.

5) Here are some examples of ways in which a market may be <u>segmented</u>:

1) <u>Age</u> — for example the teenage market, or "grey power" (the over-55s).

2) <u>Income</u> — how much different people earn will affect what they are willing to buy.

3) <u>Location</u> — try selling stottie cakes outside the North East, or jellied eels outside London.

4) <u>Gender</u> — for example, chocolate manufacturers target some items at women (e.g. Flake) and some at men (e.g. Yorkie®).

We're targeting London-based Geordies.

Jellied stottie eel cakes

Market Research is Useful to Businesses

1) Market research is really important because it helps a business to <u>understand</u> its <u>customers</u> and <u>competitors</u>. This should help a business to create a <u>good marketing mix</u>.

2) Market research means that businesses will be better able to <u>identify</u> their customers' needs and therefore be more likely to provide products that <u>satisfy</u> those needs and that customers will <u>buy</u>.

3) By <u>identifying</u> and <u>satisfying</u> customers' needs, businesses will be able to:

- <u>Increase sales</u> — the <u>demand</u> for a product or service is <u>how much</u> of it people will be <u>willing to buy</u> at a <u>given price</u>. Knowing the demand for a product can help businesses to <u>increase sales</u> by adjusting their <u>pricing</u>. It can also help them to avoid <u>costly mistakes</u>, such as making <u>too much</u> of a product.

- <u>Stay competitive</u> — gathering information on the <u>products</u> and <u>prices</u> of <u>competitors</u> can help to show how they are <u>different</u>. This can help a business to improve its <u>strategies</u> to be more <u>competitive</u>.

- <u>Create targeted marketing</u> — by understanding their target market, the business will be better able to produce <u>promotional material</u> that will be <u>effective</u> and <u>products</u> that the target market will <u>buy</u>.

I love segments — of a certain type of chocolate orange...

Businesses can't succeed without understanding their place in the market. They need to know who their customers are, what they need, and whether these needs are being met by the competition. One up for market research.

Types of Market Research

Market research can help businesses find out lots of information, including whether there's a gap in the market. To do this businesses can carry out different types of market research...

Market Research Can be Used to Find Market Opportunities

1) Sometimes a group of customers will have a need that isn't being met. This is a market opportunity. A business will want to develop a way to meet the customers' needs before its competitors do.

2) This might mean developing a new product. Or it might mean selling an existing product in a new place or at a new price, or maybe just promoting it in a new way to convince customers they need it.

3) Market research can help a business find out about any marketing opportunities that might be present.

4) The type of market research used by a business is likely to depend on things like how big it is, how much money it can afford to spend, how quickly it needs the data and how much data it needs.

Primary Research is Doing Your Own Donkey Work

1) There are two different types of market research — primary and secondary.

2) Primary research involves things like questionnaires (documents with questions that are sent to people), phone surveys (collecting information from people over the phone), interviews (asking questions face-to-face) and focus groups (where a small group of people discuss their opinions of a product).

3) It's useful for finding out new information, and getting customers' views on your products.

4) A business can't ask every potential customer for their views — they generally just ask a sample of people.

5) Large samples are the most accurate but also the most expensive. Small businesses may have to compromise here and use small sample groups to keep their costs down.

6) Businesses can also save on costs by carrying out research over the telephone or internet rather than in person — this is especially useful for small businesses.

7) Primary research provides data that's up-to-date, relevant and specific to the needs of your business. The research can also be specific to the target market.

8) But on the downside, it's expensive, and can be time-consuming.

9) Different types of primary research have different advantages and disadvantages. E.g. questionnaires are cheap and can be used to sample a large geographic area, but it's likely that many people won't respond. Phone surveys and interviews have a much higher rate of response but they can be more expensive. Focus groups are faster than interviewing several people individually, but may mean that quieter individuals do not get their opinion heard.

Secondary Research is Looking at Other People's Work

1) Secondary research gives businesses access to a wide range of data — not just the views of their sample groups. It's useful for looking at the whole market, and analysing past trends to predict the future.

2) It involves looking at things like market research reports (such as from Mintel), government publications (such as the Family Expenditure Survey or Social Trends), and articles in newspapers and magazines and on the internet.

3) It's often used by small businesses as it's cheaper than primary research, and the data is easily found and instantly available.

4) Disadvantages of secondary research are that it's not always relevant to your needs, it's not specifically about your products, and it's often out of date.

Telephone surveys — don't get hung up about them...

Market research is crucial for new businesses — they need to decide what they want to find out about the market and then choose the best method for collecting the data. Or things could go belly-up pretty quickly.

Section 5 — Marketing

Using Market Research

Businesses can use <u>sales data</u> to analyse how products sell. If a product's sales are <u>poor</u>, the <u>problem</u> might be with the <u>product</u> itself, its <u>price</u>, the way it's being <u>promoted</u>, or (you guessed it...) the <u>place</u> it's being sold. Whatever the problem, it needs to be <u>dealt with</u> before the business makes too much of a loss. No pressure...

Data Can be Quantitative or Qualitative

1) Suppose you want to do some market research about chocolate pizza. You can find out <u>two kinds</u> of information.

2) <u>Quantitative</u> information is anything you can <u>measure</u> or <u>reduce to a number</u>. Asking "How many chocolate pizzas will you buy each week?" will give a quantitative answer.

3) <u>Qualitative</u> information is all about people's <u>feelings and opinions</u>. Asking "What do you think of chocolate pizzas?" will give a qualitative answer. Qualitative data is <u>tricky</u> to analyse because it's <u>hard to compare</u> two people's opinions. However, allowing customers to voice their opinions is likely to give a <u>greater depth</u> of information.

4) Good market research will use <u>both types</u> of information.

Ohhh... sweeeet... cheesy... nom nom nom...

I'm sorry — what was the question again?

You Need to be Able to Interpret Market Research

In an exam, you could get asked to look at the <u>results</u> of some market research and come up with ideas for how a business could improve its <u>marketing mix</u> (see p.53) based on the research. E.g.

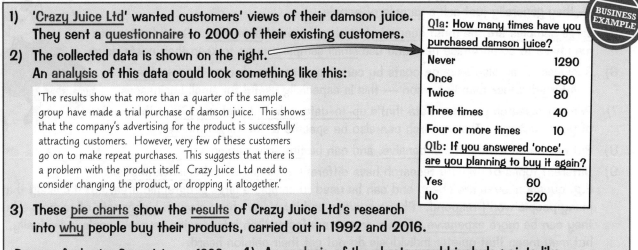

BUSINESS EXAMPLE

1) '<u>Crazy Juice Ltd</u>' wanted customers' views of their damson juice. They sent a <u>questionnaire</u> to 2000 of their existing customers.

2) The collected data is shown on the right. An <u>analysis</u> of this data could look something like this:

'The results show that more than a quarter of the sample group have made a trial purchase of damson juice. This shows that the company's advertising for the product is successfully attracting customers. However, very few of these customers go on to make repeat purchases. This suggests that there is a problem with the product itself. Crazy Juice Ltd need to consider changing the product, or dropping it altogether.'

Q1a: How many times have you purchased damson juice?	
Never	1290
Once	580
Twice	80
Three times	40
Four or more times	10
Q1b: If you answered 'once', are you planning to buy it again?	
Yes	60
No	520

3) These <u>pie charts</u> show the <u>results</u> of Crazy Juice Ltd's research into <u>why</u> people buy their products, carried out in 1992 and 2016.

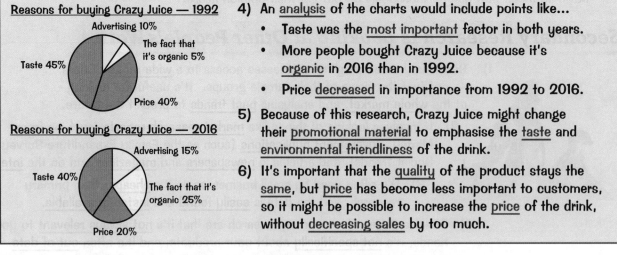

Reasons for buying Crazy Juice — 1992
Advertising 10%
The fact that it's organic 5%
Taste 45%
Price 40%

Reasons for buying Crazy Juice — 2016
Advertising 15%
The fact that it's organic 25%
Taste 40%
Price 20%

4) An <u>analysis</u> of the charts would include points like...
- Taste was the <u>most important</u> factor in both years.
- More people bought Crazy Juice because it's <u>organic</u> in 2016 than in 1992.
- Price <u>decreased</u> in importance from 1992 to 2016.

5) Because of this research, Crazy Juice might change their <u>promotional material</u> to emphasise the <u>taste</u> and <u>environmental friendliness</u> of the drink.

6) It's important that the <u>quality</u> of the product stays the <u>same</u>, but <u>price</u> has become less important to customers, so it might be possible to increase the <u>price</u> of the drink, without <u>decreasing sales</u> by too much.

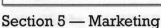
PRACTICE QUESTION

Sales analysis — go on, try it. You might like it...

Q1 Write whether the following types of data are quantitative or qualitative:
    a) sales figures for different market segments, b) reports on the quality of products from customers.

Product Life Cycles

It's back to the <u>four Ps</u> of the <u>marketing mix</u> (see p.53) and it's time to look at the <u>product</u> again. Even firms that come up with great products will find that they don't sell well <u>forever</u> — all products have a <u>life cycle</u>.

Demand for a Product Changes Over Time

All products go through the same <u>life cycle</u> — but the sales life of some products is <u>longer</u> than others'. For example, the sales life of most <u>cars</u> is about <u>ten years</u>, but the sales life of many <u>computer games</u> is only a <u>few months</u>. Whatever the product, its <u>marketing mix</u> will need to <u>change</u> during its life cycle.

1) <u>RESEARCH AND DEVELOPMENT (R&D)</u> is the first stage of a product's life cycle. It is used to develop an idea and turn it into a marketable <u>product</u>.

- <u>Scientific research</u> is often vital for product development. A lot of scientific research is done in universities. It's often "<u>pure</u>" science — without any kind of <u>commercial aim</u>.
- Large businesses often then have teams of "<u>applied</u>" scientists, who try to use recent scientific discoveries to develop <u>new</u> or <u>improved</u> products to sell.
- One aim during product development is to find the most <u>cost-effective materials</u> and <u>methods</u> to use.

2) <u>INTRODUCTION</u> comes next — the product is <u>launched</u> and put <u>on sale</u> for the first time. This is usually backed up with lots of <u>advertising</u> and <u>sales promotions</u>. <u>Place</u> is also an important P here — there's no point launching a product in places where nobody will be interested in buying it.

3) <u>GROWTH</u> — During this phase, demand <u>increases</u>, until the product becomes <u>established</u>.

4) <u>MATURITY</u> — Demand reaches its <u>peak</u> during this stage. Promotion becomes <u>less important</u> — businesses will continue to <u>advertise</u> the product, but less than at its launch. As the product's popularity <u>grows</u>, businesses will try to make the product more <u>widely available</u>. Towards the end of this phase, the market becomes <u>saturated</u> and there's <u>no more room</u> to expand.

5) <u>DECLINE</u> — Eventually demand starts to <u>fall</u> as rival products <u>take over</u>. The life cycle is linked to the <u>cash flow</u> of the business during the life of the product.

As demand (see p.54) for a product increases sales of the product will also increase, and vice versa.

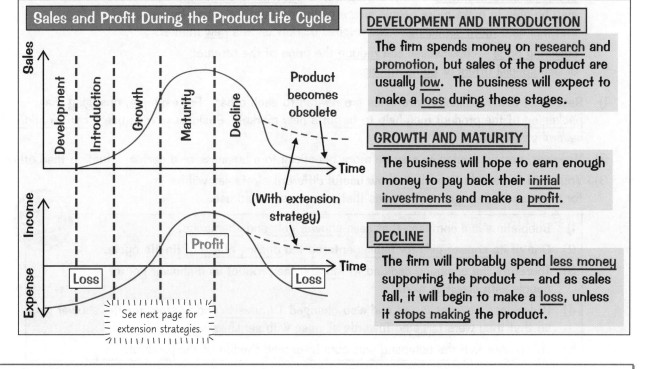

Sales and Profit During the Product Life Cycle

DEVELOPMENT AND INTRODUCTION

The firm spends money on <u>research</u> and <u>promotion</u>, but sales of the product are usually <u>low</u>. The business will expect to make a <u>loss</u> during these stages.

GROWTH AND MATURITY

The business will hope to earn enough money to pay back their <u>initial investments</u> and make a <u>profit</u>.

DECLINE

The firm will probably spend <u>less money</u> supporting the product — and as sales fall, it will begin to make a <u>loss</u>, unless it <u>stops making</u> the product.

See next page for extension strategies.

Marketing a product? Sounds more like parenting...

So, make a product that people want. Love it and nurture it throughout its life cycle. Then watch as it gets old, becomes unpopular and starts losing you money — products can be so ungrateful. Try not to cry.

Extension Strategies

Over time the sales of products may eventually <u>decline</u>, as you saw on the previous page. But that's not the end of the story — oh no. There are lots of things that businesses can do to <u>keep their products selling</u>. These are called <u>extension strategies</u> — they drag out the life of a product to the bitter end...

Firms May Try to Extend the Life of Products in Decline

1) Although the sales of all products will eventually decline, firms can take action to <u>extend their life</u>.

> Scalpel...
> needles... sale sign.
> Come on people,
> let's move — there's a
> life to extend here.

2) They might decide to use an <u>extension strategy</u> during the decline phase of the life cycle.

3) If the extension strategy works, the product will make profit for <u>longer</u>.

4) However, it means <u>spending more</u> money on the product — this <u>takes away</u> cash from other parts of the business.

5) Firms have to strike a <u>balance</u> between investing money in supporting <u>old</u> products and in designing <u>new</u> ones.

There are Several Types of Extension Strategy

There are <u>lots</u> of ways that firms can extend the life of their products, for example:

1) <u>Adding more or different features</u> — adding new features may increase <u>demand</u> for the product by making it <u>more useful</u> or <u>more appealing</u> to customers.

2) <u>Using new packaging</u> — creating a new packaging <u>design</u> for the product may make it more <u>eye-catching</u>, so that customers are more likely to <u>see</u> it and <u>choose</u> it over competitors' products. A new image for the product may also attract a <u>new target market</u>...

3) <u>Targeting new markets</u> — businesses can find new markets for their products, for example a different <u>age group</u> or <u>country</u>. They can then target their <u>promotional material</u> at the new markets to <u>extend</u> the life of the product.

4) <u>Changing advertisements</u> — by running a new <u>advertising campaign</u>, businesses may be able to make <u>more</u> people aware of the product, or promote it in a way that makes it <u>more appealing</u> to the original market or to a <u>new</u> market.

5) <u>Lowering price</u> — businesses can <u>reduce</u> the price of the product, or use <u>special offers</u> or <u>competitions</u>.

1) Several of these extension strategies are <u>related</u> to each other. For example, changing the <u>packaging</u> of the product may help to <u>target</u> a new market. Businesses may use a <u>combination</u> of several strategies.

2) However, certain strategies may be more <u>beneficial</u> to a business or a certain situation than others.

3) You need to be able to <u>evaluate</u> how useful different strategies will be for a business, or <u>suggest</u> strategies that a business could use.

BUSINESS EXAMPLE

1) Bubbletime is a company that sells <u>shower gels</u> and <u>shampoos</u>.

2) One of its <u>shower gels</u> for <u>babies</u> entered the <u>decline phase</u> of its life cycle.

3) Therefore the company decided to <u>rebrand</u> the product as a shower gel for <u>people with sensitive skin</u>.

4) It designed <u>new packaging</u> and also changed <u>TV adverts</u> and <u>posters</u> for the shower gel, so that they were <u>targeted</u> towards <u>all ages</u> with <u>sensitive skin</u>.

5) This meant that the company was able to <u>extend</u> the life of the product.

Extension Strategies — for when your homework's late...

So, instead of letting them retire gracefully, firms just keep those products working. Some people have no respect.

Product Portfolios

A firm's <u>product portfolio</u> is basically a <u>list</u> of all the products that it sells. Companies need to make marketing decisions not just for single products, but for their whole product portfolio. Tricky.

A Product Portfolio is a Range of Products

1) A <u>product portfolio</u> is the <u>range</u> of <u>different products</u> that a business sells.

2) Businesses aim to have a <u>balanced</u> product portfolio. What this means is that they ideally want to be selling a <u>variety</u> of different products, all at <u>different stages</u> of the product life cycle.

3) This means that if one product <u>fails</u>, they should still be able to depend on the others.

Boston Matrix — Market Share and Market Growth

The <u>Boston Matrix</u> (or <u>Boston Box</u>) is a way for a firm to analyse its product portfolio. The <u>market share</u> of each product is considered, as well as <u>how fast</u> the market the product is in is <u>growing</u>. Then each product is assigned a slightly silly name.

Each circle in the matrix represents one product. The size of each circle represents the revenue (see p.11) of the product.

Question marks

All <u>new</u> products are "question marks" (sometimes called "<u>problem children</u>" or "<u>wildcats</u>" — like I said, silly names). They have a <u>small market share</u> but <u>high market growth</u>. They aren't profitable yet and need <u>heavy marketing</u> to give them a chance of success.

Dogs

"Dogs" have <u>low market share</u> and <u>low market growth</u> — they're pretty much a lost cause. The business will either get what profit it can before <u>discontinuing</u> them, or <u>sell them off</u>.

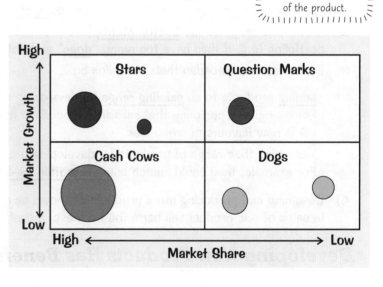

Cash cows

"Cash cows" bring in <u>plenty of money</u>. They have <u>high market share</u> but <u>low market growth</u> — they're in their maturity phase. Costs are <u>low</u>, since they've already been promoted and are produced in <u>high volumes</u>.

Stars

"Stars" have <u>high market share</u> and <u>high market growth</u> — they're future cash cows.

The Boston Matrix Helps to Analyse a Product Portfolio

1) The Boston Matrix helps a business see whether it has a <u>balanced</u> product portfolio.

2) A balanced product portfolio means that a business can use money from its <u>cash cows</u> to invest in its <u>question marks</u> so they can become <u>stars</u>.

3) The Boston Matrix has its limitations though. For example, a dog may still have <u>strong cash flow</u> and be <u>profitable despite falling sales</u> and a <u>low market share</u>.

One of the few times when selling off your dog is acceptable...

The names should be a bit of a giveaway here — you can keep 'milking' cash cows for more money, stars are doing pretty well, dogs are the pets that don't pay their own way and question marks are... well, question marks...

Product Development

It's not wise to put all your eggs in one basket — that's why businesses try to have a few <u>different</u> products on the go at the same time. That's called having a <u>broad product portfolio</u>, in business-speak...

Businesses Need a Variety of Products

I don't mean to be rude mate, but you look like you need an awful lot of investment...

1) Most large businesses will have products at <u>different stages</u> of the product life-cycle, giving them a <u>balanced portfolio</u>.

2) They'll have some products that have reached the <u>peak</u> of their sales — bringing in <u>lots of money</u> with little investment. These are responsible for most of the business's income.

3) However, at some point these products will start to <u>decline</u> and will have to be <u>replaced</u>. So the firm needs to have products in the <u>development</u> and <u>introduction</u> stages that will later grow to <u>maturity</u> and take their place. These products still need <u>lots of investment</u>.

Firms May Broaden Their Product Portfolios

1) Businesses may <u>broaden</u> (expand) their portfolios in order to <u>increase sales</u>, target a <u>different segment</u> of the market or <u>compete</u> with other companies.

2) A business may use the <u>Boston Matrix</u> (see previous page) to see if they need to broaden their portfolios (e.g. if they have too many "<u>dogs</u>" and not enough "<u>stars</u>" or "<u>cash cows</u>").

3) Businesses can broaden their portfolios by...

- <u>adding</u> products to an <u>existing range</u> by developing new products <u>based on</u> their current ones. For example, a company that sells fruit smoothies made from local produce could launch some <u>new flavours</u> of smoothies.

- increasing their range of products by developing products that are <u>different</u> from their current ones. For example, they could launch some <u>smoothie ice-lollies</u> made from locally-produced fruit.

4) Designing and producing more products is known as <u>diversification</u>. It <u>reduces the risk</u> that a decline in sales of one product will harm the business, meaning that there's less threat to the firm's <u>profits</u>.

Developing New Products Has Benefits and Risks

As well as making a business less <u>reliant</u> on a single product selling well, there are <u>other benefits</u> and also <u>risks</u> of developing new products:

Benefits	Risks
• New products will increase overall <u>sales</u> for the business and may <u>extend</u> the life-cycle of <u>existing products</u> (see p.58).	• It can be a very <u>costly</u> and <u>time-consuming</u> process — businesses risk running out of money if they invest too much into <u>research and development</u> and don't get the products to market <u>quickly enough</u>.
• They may appeal to a <u>new market segment</u> and so open up business opportunities.	
• Businesses can initially charge <u>higher prices</u> for new products before their <u>competitors</u> bring similar products to the market.	• Businesses can end up <u>wasting resources</u> by developing something customers <u>don't want</u>.
• It can be good for a firm's <u>reputation</u> — if they've been the first to launch exciting new products in the past, people will naturally be interested in their <u>future products</u>.	• Businesses might not be able to produce the new product on a <u>large scale</u> at a <u>low enough cost</u>.
	• Businesses risk ruining their reputation if the new product is of <u>poor quality</u>.

Port foalio — a harbour for young horses...

Having loads of products is no good if they're not selling well, so businesses have to be careful when they're investing in new products. There's a bit more on how they can make sure they get things right on the next page.

More on Product Development

The <u>right product</u> is the basis of all good marketing — so you have to understand the <u>target market</u>. Even then, you need to make sure the <u>brand image</u> and product <u>design</u> is good. Some people are never happy...

Be Market-Driven — Not Product-Driven

1) <u>Market-driven</u> firms will use <u>market research</u> to find out what the <u>target market wants</u>, then make it. This usually means the product is <u>useful</u> — like an MP3 player with a built-in radio.

2) <u>Product-driven</u> firms will design or invent a <u>new product</u> and then <u>try to sell it</u>. This often means they make something nobody really wants — like an MP3 player with a built-in toaster.

3) With very few exceptions, <u>market-driven</u> firms do best.

Develop a Brand Image for the Product

Having a good <u>brand image</u> is the secret to marketing success.

1) Products with a strong brand image are <u>easily recognised</u> and <u>liked</u> by customers.

2) A strong brand image is usually <u>built up</u> over a number of years. Businesses can spend a lot of money on building a positive brand image — think Coca-Cola®, BMW and Apple® Computers.

3) The brand has to be <u>constantly managed</u> using the marketing mix. <u>Products</u>, <u>prices</u>, methods of <u>promotion</u>, and <u>places</u> where they're sold all have to be right to build a positive brand image.

4) Brand image can help to increase <u>sales</u> — both first time purchases and repeat purchases. If a brand is liked and easily recognised, it will often be chosen over competing products.

5) Probably the most important element of brand image is a reputation for <u>high quality</u> products. Customers won't be loyal if products fall to pieces after a week (unless they're really, <u>really</u> cool).

Make Your Product Different from the Competition

<u>Product differentiation</u> is about making your products distinctive in the market. These differences should make customers want to buy <u>your</u> product instead of competing products.

1) Without product differentiation, customers will think your product is <u>identical</u> to others. They'll have no reason to buy it unless it's <u>cheaper</u> — which means less profit for you.

2) One way to achieve this is to give the product a <u>unique selling point</u> (USP). This is some feature that makes it different to its <u>competitors</u> (e.g. a special feature).

3) <u>Product design</u> is also hugely important for product differentiation. The <u>design mix</u> has three main ingredients:

<u>Function</u> — the design must be fit for its <u>purpose</u>. A car without an engine would be a non-starter. <u>Unique features</u> can also help — a razor with seven blades shaves better than a razor with one. Probably.

<u>Cost</u> — a good design will lead to <u>low manufacturing costs</u>. This means <u>higher profits</u>.

<u>Appearance</u> — a good product should look <u>attractive</u> and <u>distinctive</u>. <u>Packaging</u> can also help a product to <u>stand out</u> (and protect it till it reaches the customer).

USP — Underwater Serving Plates — for the unique dinner party

Q1 A business that specialises in dog food products decides to create a new cat food product. Discuss the issues that the business will need to consider in order to be successful with the new product.

Price

Time for another of those <u>P's</u> now and it's the one that <u>customers</u> usually think is <u>most important</u> — <u>price</u>.

Businesses Need to Think About Demand When Setting Prices

1) Most businesses aim to make a <u>profit</u> — this means that the <u>money</u> they get from <u>selling</u> their products has to be <u>more</u> than the business's <u>costs</u>.

2) The easiest way to do this is to make the <u>price</u> of <u>each product higher</u> than the <u>total cost</u> of making it.

> The total cost of making a product includes the cost of getting it to market too — e.g. marketing and distribution costs.

3) However, firms need to think about how the price of a product will affect <u>demand</u> (the quantity of a product that customers are <u>able</u> and <u>willing</u> to buy). As <u>prices rise</u>, <u>demand</u> for a product tends to <u>fall</u>. So firms need to make sure that the price of a product isn't <u>so high</u> that they <u>won't sell</u> many.

4) Sometimes, a firm may need to set the price of a product <u>lower</u> than the total cost of making it so that there is still a <u>decent level</u> of demand for the product (see next page). In this case the firm may have to rely on making lots of profit on <u>other products</u> in its portfolio so that it doesn't go bust.

Internal and External Factors Influence Pricing Decisions

There are <u>many factors</u> to consider when deciding on the price of a product. Some of these factors are <u>internal</u> (controlled by the business) and some are <u>external</u> (not controlled by the business).

Internal

- A business's <u>aims and objectives</u> will influence its prices. E.g. if a business is aiming to <u>increase</u> its <u>market share</u>, it might put its prices <u>lower</u> than its <u>competitors'</u> to <u>increase sales</u>. Or if the business is aiming to <u>expand</u>, it might price in a way that <u>maximises profits</u> so it can <u>fund</u> the expansion.

- A business's <u>internal costs</u> may change, which can affect its prices. For example, it might invest in some new machinery which is <u>cheaper to run</u>, so its costs <u>fall</u> in the long term. This means it can afford to <u>charge less</u> for its products and still make a <u>profit</u>.

- Where a product is in its <u>life cycle</u> will affect its price. For example, when the product is in the <u>introduction</u> and <u>growth</u> phases a firm may charge a <u>very low</u> or <u>very high</u> price to encourage people to buy it (see next page). When it's in the <u>maturity</u> phase, a firm may need to bring its price in line with <u>competitors' prices</u> (see below). When it's in the <u>decline</u> phase, the firm may need to <u>reduce</u> the price in order to increase demand for the product again.

- Other elements of the <u>marketing mix</u> will also influence pricing. For example, if a business is trying to <u>promote</u> a product its price may be <u>reduced</u> for a period.

External

- The <u>nature of the market</u> that a product is in will affect its price. For example, if the product is aimed at a <u>high-end</u>, <u>luxury</u> market, its price will be <u>higher</u> than a similar product aimed at a less luxurious market.

- If the product is sold in a <u>competitive</u> market, the firm needs to look at what <u>competitors are charging</u> for similar products. If a firm puts its prices <u>too high</u>, <u>customers</u> will just choose a <u>competitor's</u> product. If it puts its prices <u>too low</u>, customers will <u>query</u> whether the <u>quality is as good</u> as its competitors'.

> There's more on the next page about how competitors affect a firm's prices.

- A business doesn't have control over all of its <u>costs</u> (e.g. the cost of raw materials). If these <u>go up</u> a business may have to <u>increase</u> its prices.

A business's pricing decisions are likely to change as it <u>grows</u>. For example, once it has developed <u>loyal customers</u> and a <u>good reputation</u>, it might be able to <u>increase</u> prices without demand falling too much. On the other hand, as a business grows it can benefit from <u>economies of scale</u> (see page 14). This means that the <u>average cost</u> of making each product <u>falls</u>, so the business can afford to <u>lower</u> its prices.

You can't put a price on happiness...

...but you can make examiners happy by knowing the different factors that affect a business's prices.

Pricing Strategies

This is where bosses narrow their eyes and stroke their chins — they need to choose the best <u>pricing strategy</u>.

There are Five Pricing Strategies You Need to Know About

1) Price Penetration

1) This is where a firm charges a very <u>low</u> price when a product is <u>new</u> to get lots of people to <u>try it</u>.
2) It's a good way to establish a <u>market share</u> for a product in a <u>competitive market</u>.
3) The product will make <u>very little profit</u> at first but once it has become <u>established</u> the firm <u>increases</u> the price. Loyal customers should <u>continue</u> to buy the product despite the price increase.

2) Loss Leader Pricing

1) This is when the price of a product is set <u>below cost</u>. The firm doesn't make a profit on it, but the idea is that customers will <u>buy other products as well</u> (which it does make a profit on).
2) E.g. <u>games consoles</u> are often priced <u>below cost</u> but firms make <u>profit</u> on <u>games</u> that go with them.

3) Price Skimming

It may sound steep, but this is cutting-edge technology.

1) This is where firms charge a <u>high price</u> to begin with — they can usually do this when they know there will be a <u>high demand</u> for the product (e.g. goods that use <u>new technology</u> and have a desirable <u>USP</u>, such as smart TVs).
2) It often works for <u>established firms</u> as they'll have <u>loyal customers</u> who will be <u>willing to pay</u>.
3) The high price helps the firm to <u>increase revenue</u> and to cover any <u>research and development</u> costs.
4) Having a high price also helps to make the product more <u>desirable</u> to people with <u>high incomes</u>, which can help to improve the firm's <u>image</u>.
5) Once the product's <u>established</u>, the firm <u>lowers the price</u> to help it become a <u>mass-market</u> product.

4) Competitive Pricing

1) This is where the firm has to charge <u>similar</u> prices to <u>other firms</u>.
2) It happens most when there is <u>lots of choice</u> and not much product differentiation — e.g. petrol.
3) The firm may make <u>very little profit</u> and have to find ways <u>other than price</u> to <u>attract</u> customers.

5) Cost-Plus Pricing

Firms may use this method if they're <u>not</u> in <u>price competition</u> with other producers. The firm works out the <u>total cost</u> of making the product, and then adds on a certain amount depending on how much <u>profit</u> they want to make while still having reasonable <u>demand</u>. There are <u>two main ways</u> it can be done:

Using a Mark-Up

Work out how much the product costs and then add a <u>percentage mark-up</u>. So if the product costs <u>£2</u> to make, and you want a 25% mark-up, you'd sell it for £2 + 25% = £2.50.

Using a Profit Margin

Work out how much the product costs and increase it to get the <u>profit margin</u> you want. So if the product costs <u>£2</u> to make, and you want a <u>20% profit margin</u>, this means that £2 is 80% of your required selling price. So 80% = 200p, 1% = 200 ÷ 80 = 2.5p, 100% = 2.5p × 100 = 250p. So you'd sell it for <u>£2.50</u>.

Note: mark-up is expressed as a % of <u>cost</u>. Profit margin is expressed as a % of the <u>selling price</u>.

Price skimming — getting 99p to hop across a pond's surface...

Q1 A supermarket sells its own-brand steak pies for less than it costs to make them. Name the type of pricing strategy the supermarket is using and suggest why it uses this strategy.

Methods of Promotion

Promotion is basically when firms big-up a product so that customers notice it and want to buy it.

Promotion is Really Important for a Business

Firms spend lots of time and money on promotion. There are many reasons why they do it:

1) To inform customers about the product — customers need to know that the product exists, what it is or does and what its USP is. Even if it's been on the market for some time, customers may still need reminding about a product.

2) To persuade customers to buy the product — firms have to make customers really want the product and to choose it over competitors' products. Firms use many different tactics to do this, such as tempting descriptions, displaying positive results of customer surveys, and special offers.

3) To create or change the image of a product — for example, the use of humour and bold colours creates a fun and vibrant image, whereas darker colours and classical music might create a more sophisticated, luxurious image. The image that a firm wants a product to have will largely depend on who it's aimed at.

Chipper's Chip Shop
Much better than that
other chip shop just down
there — they're rubbish.

4) To create or increase sales — this one is usually the ultimate reason for promotion — more sales can lead to more profit and a greater market share.

Firms Promote Their Products by Advertising

Advertising is any message that a firm pays for which promotes the firm or its products.
There are many different ways that a firm may choose to advertise. For example:

1) NEWSPAPERS — local ones are good for reaching a specific geographical area and national ones are good for reaching a wide audience. They're printed often so they're a good way to promote temporary offers. However, the print quality is usually poor and the number of people reading newspapers is declining.

2) MAGAZINES are good for targeting specialist markets over a wide area. Magazine adverts can be pricier than newspaper adverts, but they're better quality and people tend to hang on to magazines for longer.

3) POSTERS and BILLBOARDS can be placed near a target audience, stay in place for a long time and be seen daily by lots of people. But people might not look at them for long, so messages need to be short.

4) LEAFLETS, FLYERS and BUSINESS CARDS are cheap to produce and distribute. They can be targeted at certain areas and people can keep them until they need the information. But many people see them as 'junk' and throw them away quickly.

5) TELEVISION adverts can be seen by a wide audience and include sounds and moving images. They can deliver long messages and help to emphasise the firm's image. On the downside, they're very expensive.

6) INTERNET adverts can be seen at any time by a large, targeted audience, can include sounds and moving images, and customers can visit the firm's website immediately after viewing the advert. However, there are so many adverts online, people may stop looking at them properly or choose to block them.

Businesses Can Sponsor Organisations and Events

Firms sometimes give money to organisations and events — e.g. schools, TV production firms and exhibitions. In return, their name is displayed by the organisation or at the event. This is called sponsorship. E.g.:

• SPORT — A large firm might stamp its brand name all over an international competition. A smaller firm might only be able to afford to sponsor the local Sunday League team, but the aim is the same.

• TELEVISION — Some soap operas and weather reports are sponsored by well-known brands.

Sponsorship can create a high profile for your business or brand name. But if the thing you're sponsoring starts to get bad publicity, your company's image might suffer too.

I LOVE getting people to move about — yep, I'm totally pro-motion...

Promotion's crucial, especially in a very competitive market. There are more methods of promotion coming up...

More Methods of Promotion

So you've learnt about advertising and sponsorship — now here are another three methods of promotion...

Public Relations (PR) Gets a Firm Noticed in the Media

1) PR involves communicating with the media, e.g. doing a TV interview or issuing a press release.

2) It can be a cheap and easy way to get a firm noticed by a wide audience.

3) But once the firm has spoken to the media, it has little control over what the public get to see or hear. E.g. the full TV interview might not be shown or journalists may use the press release to criticise the firm's activities.

A press release is a piece of writing about a firm's activities (e.g. the launch of a new product), which is sent to the media in the hope that they will run a story on it.

Sales Promotion is a Short-Term Method Used to Boost Sales

1) You need to know these six sales promotion methods that firms use:

- competitions
- 2 for 1 offers
- free samples
- coupons, e.g. 20p off a product
- point of sale displays, e.g. a branded display case at the front of a shop
- free gifts, e.g. a cuddly toy that comes with the product

2) An advantage of sales promotion is that it should encourage new customers to try a product. This will boost sales in the short term but could also increase sales in the long term if customers like the product and continue to buy it once the promotion has ended.

3) A disadvantage of sales promotion is that customers get used to seeing products on promotion and may be reluctant to buy them at other times. Also, using regular sales promotions might make a product feel like less of a luxury item, so some customers looking for luxury might be put off buying it.

Firms Can Use Social Media to Promote Products

1) Social media is a quick, easy and cheap way for firms to promote their products.

2) Firms can use their social media pages to do things like advertise products, offer sales promotions, share news stories about their products and build up excitement for new products being launched.

3) They can add information whenever they like, so they can respond quickly to internal or external changes.

4) Customers can go quickly from the social media page to the firm's website where they can buy products.

5) However, any mistakes or negative customer comments can be seen quickly by lots of people, so time and money needs to be spent carefully monitoring the site.

Firms Must Choose the Best Promotional Mix

Firms use a combination of different promotional methods (advertising, sponsorship, PR, etc.) to promote a product — this is called the promotional mix. You need to be able to analyse the different factors that might influence a firm's promotional mix. Here are some things you should think about:

1) **Finance available:** E.g. large firms can usually afford to spend more than smaller ones.

2) **Nature of the product or service:** E.g. some products need lots of description to say what they are.

3) **What competitors are doing:** E.g. a firm might want to use social media if all of its competitors are.

4) **Nature of the market:** E.g. if a market is growing rapidly, a firm may be willing to spend more on promotion as they are predicting a large increase in sales, which will cover the costs.

5) **Target market:** promotions might need to be in a place where they'll be seen by the right people, and need to be presented in a way that they'll appeal to the right people.

A sturdy pair of rocket boots — another way to boost sales...

Firms need people to know about them and their products. You should know the pros and cons of the promotional methods covered here and on the previous page — advertising, sponsorship, PR, sales promotions and social media.

Place

Place (the final P) is all about channels of distribution — how products get from manufacturers to consumers.

Firms Need to Choose the Most Suitable Channel of Distribution

1) Firms need to make sure that their products are available to consumers at the right place. To do this, they need to choose the most appropriate channel of distribution. This depends on things like where the consumer is likely to shop, how many consumers they want their products to reach, how quickly they want the product to get to the consumer, and how much customer service the consumer will need.

2) Channels of distribution can include wholesalers (these buy products in bulk and store them in a warehouse), retailers (these sell products to consumers) and telesales (this means selling products to consumers via phone). Here are three common channels of distribution:

1) Selling to wholesalers

Manufacturers sell products to a wholesaler, then consumers or retailers buy the products from the wholesaler (e.g. from a cash and carry warehouse). This channel is good for manufacturers that make lots of a particular product and don't need to communicate much with the consumer — e.g. a baked beans manufacturer. Selling to a wholesaler means the manufacturer gets bulk orders and doesn't have to store lots of stock. The wholesaler will already have customers, so products can reach lots of potential consumers quickly. And if retailers buy from the wholesaler, it means the product will end up being sold in even more places, so reach even more customers. The problem with this channel is that consumers may get lower levels of customer service compared to the other channels.

Wholesalers and retailers need to make a profit, which can push up prices for consumers.

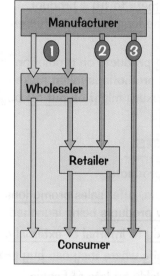

2) Selling directly to retailers

Selling directly to retailers means that the manufacturer can provide the retailer with product knowledge so the retailer can provide better customer service. So the customers have higher satisfaction with the products. The retailer can help to promote products (e.g. with point of sale displays), which may help to increase sales. Also, using retailers means that products are sold in more places, so more potential customers are exposed to them (especially if the retailer already sells similar products). However, it can be hard for new firms to persuade many retailers to stock their products.

3) Selling directly to consumers

Internet shopping, mail order and factory outlets are also examples of this channel.

This can be done via telesales. It's often the cheapest channel for the consumer. But it can be time-consuming for firms to sell products to individual customers, especially if each customer only buys small quantities. They also have to arrange delivery of the goods, which can be difficult and expensive if the customers are in lots of different places. This channel is good for firms who don't have loads of customers or firms selling one-off items, e.g. custom-made wedding dresses.

---

1) **New Twists Ltd.** are a new, small frozen food manufacturer. They are trying to decide the most appropriate channel of distribution for their products.

2) It will be difficult and expensive to sell directly to consumers — they'd have to find lots of customers, each order is only likely to be small, and frozen food needs to be delivered quickly.

3) It would be good if they could sell to big retailers as they would reach lots of consumers, but as they are a small, new firm it may be difficult to persuade large retailers to stock their products.

4) It may be best if they sell to wholesalers, as this will reduce their delivery costs but still allow their products to reach a wide range of consumers.

BUSINESS EXAMPLE

50% off all HD 50 inch LCD Smart TVs — now that's telesales...

In our modern internety world, more and more firms are cutting out the middlemen and selling directly to consumers.

E-Commerce

Finally, a page you probably already know lots about — internet shopping.

Buying and Selling Online is Called E-Commerce

E-commerce allows goods and services to be bought on the internet — and it's growing fast.

1) Firms put details of their products on their website. Customers may be directed straight to the product they want if they follow a link placed elsewhere, e.g. in an advert. Alternatively they can use the website to browse through the product range or use a search box to find the products they want.

2) Products are ordered online and are usually paid for using a credit or debit card or with PayPal.

3) The products are then delivered to the customer.

PayPal is an online payments system.

M-Commerce is Also Growing Rapidly

1) M-commerce (mobile commerce) allows goods and services to be bought using a wireless mobile device, such as a smartphone or tablet.

2) It's pretty much the same as e-commerce (customers can find and buy products on the internet), but the fact that they can do this in a wider range of locations and situations is making m-commerce more and more popular.

Customers often prefer to use a firm's app on a mobile device rather than their website.

Businesses Can Reach International Markets More Easily

Sheila Bossman's foolproof e-commerce strategy.

The internet means that people in more places can buy a business's products.

1) The internet can be accessed all over the world. As part of its marketing strategy, a business may want to target markets in foreign countries with online promotions.

2) Even small companies can do this, since it's much cheaper than buying advertising space in foreign newspapers, magazines, etc.

3) For all businesses, selling to international markets may lead to higher profits.

E-Commerce and M-Commerce are Becoming More Important

1) The internet is always growing — more and more businesses are creating websites.

2) Likewise, the number of consumers using the internet is increasing — more people have access to the internet (either at home or on a mobile device) and improvements in technology mean the service is becoming more reliable.

3) As a result, an increasing number of people are turning to the internet to buy products.

4) Businesses need to keep up with this changing trend — they need to make sure they can meet the changing expectations of customers and adapt to changing competition within the market.

Higher Customer Expectations

1) Customers expect to be able to buy products from a firm online. If they can't, it's often easy to find an online competitor selling what they want.

2) They also want things like low prices, free delivery and returns, and a website that's easy to use. If they can't get these, it's often easy for them to shop elsewhere.

More Competition

1) Customers can buy products from firms around the world, so there are a lot more firms to compete with.

2) It's easy for customers to go from one firm's website to another, so it's easy for them to compare products and prices. Therefore firms need to work harder to persuade customers to buy from them.

Customers always click with internet shopping...

When it comes to marketing, e-commerce has given firms access to places that would previously have been out of their reach. If a business wants to stay competitive in modern markets, e-commerce is the way forward.

More on E-Commerce

There are loads of good reasons to use e-commerce and m-commerce, but selling online isn't always easy.

E-Commerce and M-Commerce Have Many Advantages

E-commerce has some big advantages over traditional methods of doing business —
mostly to do with increasing sales, reducing costs and prices, and becoming more competitive.

1) A big advantage of e-commerce is that businesses can access wider markets — e.g. markets in other parts of the world. This means businesses have more potential customers, so sales may increase.

Download complete.

Oof.

2) The growth of m-commerce also means that a business's sales may increase further, as it's becoming easier for customers to buy products online.

3) E-commerce saves money on paper. Things like sales brochures and product information no longer need to be printed and posted by the firm — they can be viewed online, on apps, or downloaded by the customer.

4) Some firms that traditionally employed staff to sell products over the telephone have been able to cut costs by making these people redundant and allowing customers to buy online instead.

> • In 2004, British Airways closed two of its call centres in the UK.
> • In the two years before the decision was made, British Airways had seen a 34% decrease in calls to its call centres, as people were booking more flights online.
> • British Airways predicted that closing the call centres would save them more than £10 million within five years.

BUSINESS EXAMPLE

5) Businesses that sell successfully online may be able to close (or not have to open) high street shops. This saves the business money on things such as property and staff costs.

6) If firms rely more on online sales than sales from customers visiting their shop, they may be able to locate in more remote areas where wages tend to be lower.

7) All these savings mean that firms which only sell goods or services online can offer lower prices than high street shops — this is one of the main reasons that sales from many internet shopping sites are increasing.

There are Some Drawbacks of E-Commerce and M-Commerce

There are plenty of benefits to a firm of selling over the internet, but it's not completely straightforward. Setting up the facilities needed for e-commerce can be expensive and time-consuming.

1) Special equipment may need to be bought and installed, especially for large businesses with many customers. (A sole trader may be able to launch a website from their home computer with no problems.)

2) Firms may need to employ specialist website or app designers, who'll have to be paid. Other staff might need to be trained in using the equipment and in providing good customer service.

3) Some consumers are reluctant to buy online — they might not have internet access, or they might prefer to visit a shop where they can see what they're getting. As a result, firms might have to spend more on marketing to try to persuade more people to use their online services.

PRACTICE QUESTION

Eee, commerce — what a big decision it is...

Q1 Glitter and Sparkle Time (GAST) sell jewellery. They have two high street shops and also sell goods through their website. In the future, they are planning on closing the high street shops and only selling goods online. Some of GAST's customers have said they're disappointed about this decision.
a) Explain one reason why only selling online will mean GAST can offer its customers lower prices.
b) Suggest one reason why some customers are disappointed with GAST's decision.
c) GAST will need to improve their e-commerce services before they close their high street shops. Explain why this is likely to be an expensive process for them.

Case Study — Marketing

There's no denying it — there's a lot to learn in this section. See how well you can apply what you've learned about the world of marketing by reading this real-life case study and answering the questions.

Business Report: Marketing

Nestlé®

Nestlé® is a multinational food and drink manufacturing company. It has many different breakfast cereal products in its portfolio. It sells its cereals directly to large retailers as well as to wholesalers. However, sales of breakfast cereals are falling in the UK. This is thought to be due in part to consumers becoming concerned about the high levels of sugar in some cereals and opting for breakfast choices with a higher protein content.

Nestlé® produce Shreddies, which are one of the firm's most popular brands of cereal. Since 2007, scenes of older ladies appearing to knit Shreddies have been used in television adverts as well as on other promotional material for Shreddies. Due to the popularity of the 'Knitting Nanas', Nestlé® created an official 'Knitting Nanas' Facebook® page. On the page they encouraged people to post pictures and videos to find a new Knitting Nana. This was hugely popular and the page obtained over 250 000 fans.

Nestlé® is constantly adjusting its marketing mix. For example, in 2016, Nestlé® launched Shreddies Max, which is a granola based cereal labelled as being a good source of protein. It also redesigned some of its cereal boxes so that the price is clearly displayed. This decision was influenced by the findings of research agencies. For example, 'him!' (a research and consulting firm), found that 82% of people shopping in a convenience store would specifically look for products in the shop that had the price marked on the packaging.

Case Study Questions

Now you've read the case study, get your best marketing hat on and have a go at the following questions.

1) Suggest two reasons why Nestlé® sells to wholesalers and retailers rather than directly to consumers.
2) Explain whether the decision to promote Shreddies using the 'Knitting Nanas' television adverts was appropriate for the business and analyse the impact the campaign is likely to have had on sales.
3) Explain what Shreddies Max would be called in the Boston Matrix at the time it was launched.
4) Explain two reasons why Nestlé® may have decided to launch Shreddies Max as a new product.
5) Analyse the firm's decision to print the price on the packaging of some of its cereals.

Where does Santa eat his Shreddies? In Nestlé®...

Ho ho ho — that one's a cracker. Answering these case study questions takes a lot of writing and I know you'll be tempted to skip them — but you're bound to get asked about a case study in the exam, so it's all good practice.

Revision Summary

Well, that was quite a fun section. You learnt how hard businesses work to make sure us customers will buy products from them. But do you know your cash cows from your question marks? It's time to find out...

1) What are the four elements of the marketing mix?

2) Why is a firm's marketing mix for a product likely to change over time?

3) Why might a firm want to segment a market when conducting market research?

4) Give four different ways of segmenting a market.

5) Give three benefits to a business of identifying and satisfying customer needs.

6) What is the main difference between primary market research and secondary market research?

7) Give four methods of primary market research.

8) Give two methods of secondary market research.

9) Would a small firm be more likely to use primary or secondary market research? Explain your answer.

10) What is the difference between quantitative and qualitative market research?

11) What is the first stage in a product life cycle?

12) Explain how the marketing mix for a product will be different when it's in the introduction stage of its life cycle compared to when it's in the maturity stage.

13) Sketch a graph to show how sales of a product are likely to change throughout its life cycle.

14) What is the purpose of an extension strategy?

15) Give five different types of extension strategy.

16) What is a firm's 'product portfolio'?

17) Sketch a diagram to show the Boston Matrix. Label each box and the bottom and side of the diagram.

18) Give two ways in which a firm might broaden its product portfolio.

19) State three benefits to a firm of developing a new product.

20) State three risks involved in developing a new product.

21) Explain why it's important that a firm develops a strong brand image for a product.

22) Other than brand image, how else can a firm make sure its product is different from a competitor's?

23) Explain how a firm's costs will influence the price it charges for a product.

24) Give three internal factors that will influence a firm's pricing decisions.

25) Describe the main features of each of the following pricing strategies:
    a) price penetration,   b) price skimming,   c) competitive pricing,   d) cost-plus pricing.

26) Explain two reasons why firms choose to promote their products.

27) Give one argument for and one argument against choosing to advertise in a magazine rather than in a newspaper.

28) How can firms use sponsorship for promotion?

29) Give one advantage and one disadvantage of a firm using PR as a method of promotion.

30) List six sales promotion methods a firm might use to boost sales.

31) Give three benefits to a firm of using social media as a method of promotion.

32) What is a 'channel of distribution'?

33) Give an advantage of a manufacturer selling to a wholesaler rather than directly to consumers.

34) What is 'm-commerce'?

35) Explain why the use of e-commerce and m-commerce is becoming more important for firms.

36) Give three ways in which the use of e-commerce might reduce a firm's costs.

Sources of Finance — Small Firms

You need to know about the different sources of money for firms and some of the pros and cons of each.

Firms Need Finance for Five Reasons

1) New firms need start-up capital (the money or assets needed to set up a business).

2) New firms often have poor initial cash flow — this means that they find it hard to cover their costs (see p.11), so they need additional finance to cover this.

3) Sometimes customers delay payment, so finance is needed to cover this shortfall in (lack of) liquidity.

4) If a business is struggling, it may need additional finance to meet its day-to-day running costs.

5) Firms may need finance in order to expand — e.g. to buy larger premises.

Liquidity is how easily the business can access cash — see page 82.

Small Firms Have Several Sources of Start-up Finance

Small firms may be given money in the form of government grants.

1) **GOVERNMENT GRANTS** are often given to qualifying new or small firms. Unlike loans, they don't have to be repaid. However, there are fewer options than for loans, strict criteria may have to be met to qualify for them, and the money may have to be spent in a specific way.

Short-term sources will lend money for a limited period of time. Examples of short-term sources include:

2) **TRADE CREDIT** — businesses may give firms one or two months to pay for certain purchases. This is useful for a small firm as they have time to earn the money needed to pay the debt. However, if the firm makes the payment too late, they could end up with a large fee.

3) **OVERDRAFTS** — these let the firm take more money out of its bank account than it has paid into it. Overdrafts can allow businesses to make payments on time even if they don't have enough cash. However, they usually have a higher interest rate than other loans and the bank can cancel the overdraft at any time. If it isn't paid off, then the bank can take some of the business's assets.

Assets are valuable items owned by the business (e.g. equipment, buildings), or money owed to the business.

Long-term sources lend money for longer periods, usually more than one year. They are paid back in regular instalments over a fixed time period. This is good for businesses' cash flow. These sources include:

4) **LOANS** — there are three types of loans a small business might take out:

  • Bank loans are quick and easy to take out. Like with overdrafts, they are repaid with interest, and if they aren't repaid, the bank can repossess the firm's assets. However, the interest rate for loans is usually lower than for overdrafts.

  • It may be easier to get loans from friends and family (or to use your own savings) than from a bank. The money lent will go into the business immediately, but the individual may expect a share in the profits of the business — e.g. by forming a partnership (see p.5).

  • Mortgages are loans used to finance buying property. The property is used as collateral — this means that the property can be taken by the bank if the individual can't pay off the mortgage. Interest payments are relatively low compared to other sources of finance. A sole trader might use their own house as collateral to borrow money — they risk losing their home if their business fails.

5) **HIRE PURCHASES** — these are when a firm purchases something by first paying a deposit, then paying the rest in installments over a period of time, while they have use of the product. This allows firms to purchase useful things for their business that they otherwise couldn't afford, such as expensive machinery. It also means that they have use of the product over a longer period of time.

Movies have the highest interest rate — everybody's looking at them...

Lots of facts on this page — make sure you can write down every source of finance for a small firm and try to remember one problem with each. Learn, cover the page and start scribbling.

Sources of Finance — Established Firms

Established firms are less likely to go bankrupt. This means that they are less risky for banks to lend money to than smaller firms. They also have a few other sources of finance they can use. Alright for some...

Established Firms Have Other Sources of Funds Available

As well as the sources on the previous page, established firms can use these methods to get funds:

1) **RETAINED PROFITS** — these are profits that the owners have decided to plough back into the business after they've paid themselves a dividend (see p.10). But larger companies (e.g. PLCs — see page 6) are under pressure from shareholders to give large dividends, reducing the profit they can retain.

2) **FIXED ASSETS** — firms can raise cash by selling fixed assets (assets that a business keeps long-term, e.g. machinery/buildings) that are no longer in use. There's a limit to how many assets you can sell, though — sell too many and you can't go on trading.

3) **NEW SHARE ISSUES** — a limited company (see page 6) can issue more shares (these give the individuals that buy them part ownership in the company). The money raised does not have to be repaid to shareholders — but more shares means less control for the existing owners, and the new shareholders will also expect to be paid dividends.

Finance can be Classed as Internal or External

1) Internal finance comes from inside the business. It can be a quick and easy way to get money. It saves borrowing and having to pay back interest. However, some businesses may not have enough and have to find external sources instead.

2) External finance comes from outside the business. It usually needs to be paid back (e.g. loans) — sometimes with high interest.

Your internal finances aren't looking too great.

Internal Sources include...	External Sources include...
• Personal or business savings • Retained profits • Selling fixed assets	• Bank loans, overdrafts and mortgages • Loans from family and friends • New share issues • Trade credit • Government grants • Hire purchases

Four Factors Affect the Choice of Finance

1) Size and type of company — not all companies have access to all types of finance:
   • Some types of business may not have fixed assets available to sell.
   • Small businesses are unable to issue new shares and may also find it hard to get loans or overdrafts.

2) Amount of money needed — a company wouldn't issue more shares to buy a toaster. Small amounts of money usually come from internal sources. For larger amounts of money (e.g. for new property or machinery), the firm is more likely to need an external source of finance.

3) Length of time the finance is needed for — it'd be daft to take out a mortgage because a customer is a week late paying an invoice. Using savings or an arranged overdraft from a bank are common ways to see a business through a short-term lack of finance.

4) Cost of the finance — some sources, e.g. bank loans and overdrafts, are more expensive than others as the money has to be paid back with interest.

Overdraft — it's when the top of the door doesn't fit...

Examiners love to test whether you can identify the right source of finance to meet the needs of a business. So make sure you know the factors that affect which source of finance a firm will choose — gotta keep 'em happy...

Investments

Businesses have to keep <u>investing</u> in <u>people</u> and <u>other things</u> to keep expanding. But they must be very <u>careful</u> to make sure they don't go spending <u>too much money</u>. That's where the <u>ARR</u> comes in...

Businesses Have to Make Investments

1) <u>An investment</u> is money which is put into a business to make <u>improvements</u> in order to make the business <u>more profitable</u>.

2) Here are a few examples of investments that businesses may make:

- <u>New machinery</u> — buying new machinery may make processes <u>more efficient</u>, or may enable a business to make <u>new products</u>.
- <u>New buildings</u> — new, larger premises will enable a business to <u>expand</u> by increasing the <u>number of employees</u> it can have, the <u>amount of machinery</u> it can keep or the amount of <u>stock</u> it can <u>store</u>.
- <u>New vehicles</u> — businesses that rely on vehicles, e.g. delivery services, can expand by buying <u>more vehicles</u>, or by getting larger vehicles that can transport <u>more products</u>.

3) But <u>spending money</u> can be risky as the investment may not bring in more money to the business, and may even result in a <u>loss of money</u>.

4) So businesses often want to make sure that their investments are <u>worthwhile</u>.

5) To do this, they calculate the <u>return</u> on an investment...

You Can Find the Average Rate of Return on an Investment

1) The <u>return</u> on an investment is how much a business <u>makes</u> or <u>loses</u> as a <u>proportion</u> of the <u>original investment</u> that it puts in.

> An investment's lifespan is the length of time over which it earns money for the firm.

2) You need to be able to work out the <u>average rate of return</u> (<u>ARR</u>).

3) The average rate of return is a calculation of the <u>average return</u> on an investment over its <u>lifespan</u>.

4) To calculate it you can use this nifty <u>formula</u>:

$$\text{ARR (\%)} = \frac{\text{Average annual profit}}{\text{Initial investment}} \times 100$$

And, just to be nice, here's a worked example of how to use it:

BUSINESS EXAMPLE

The table below shows the <u>investment</u> that a business made in a project that lasted 5 years. It also shows the <u>profit</u> the business made <u>each year</u> as a result of the investment.
Calculate the <u>average rate of return</u> (<u>ARR</u>) for the investment.

	Profit				
Investment	Yr 1	Yr 2	Yr 3	Yr 4	Yr 5
(£10m)	£4m	£5m	£6m	£7m	£5m

1) First calculate the <u>total profit</u> of the project — this is the sum of the profit made by the project each year minus the cost of the <u>initial investment</u>: 4 + 5 + 6 + 7 + 5 – 10 = <u>£17m</u>

2) Then divide the total profit of the project by its lifespan in years to find the <u>average annual profit</u>: 17m ÷ 5 = <u>£3.4m</u>

3) Next, you use the <u>formula</u> above to find the <u>ARR</u>:

$$\text{ARR (\%)} = \frac{\text{average annual profit}}{\text{initial investment}} \times 100 = \frac{3.4}{10} \times 100 = 34\%$$

My average rate of return to the fridge is about 20 minutes...

Q1 Calculate the average rate of return for a project in which a company invests £14m and earns back a total of £26m over three years.

Break-Even Analysis

Break-even analysis is how companies work out at what point they will cover their costs.
Before we go into how this works, you need to recap some pesky terminology.

You Need to Recap Some Basic Financial Terms

For more on these financial terms, flick back to page 11.

1) <u>Revenue</u> — this is the amount of money that the business <u>earns</u>.
2) <u>Costs</u> — this is the amount of money that the business has to <u>spend</u>.
3) <u>Profit</u> — this is the money <u>left over</u> after costs are <u>taken away</u> (profit = revenue − costs).
4) <u>Loss</u> — when <u>costs</u> are <u>greater</u> than <u>revenue</u> the business makes a loss — they <u>lose money</u>.
5) Costs can be broken down into <u>different parts</u>:

- <u>Fixed costs</u> are costs that <u>don't change</u> with output, e.g. the cost of renting a building.
- <u>Variable costs</u> are costs that will <u>increase</u> as <u>output increases</u>, e.g. the cost of raw materials.
- <u>Total costs</u> are the <u>fixed costs plus</u> the <u>variable costs</u>.

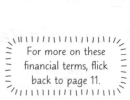

Breaking Even Means Covering Your Costs

1) The <u>break-even output</u> is the level of output where the firm will <u>just cover its costs</u>.
2) If it sells <u>more</u>, it'll make a <u>profit</u> — if it sells <u>less</u>, it'll make a <u>loss</u>.
3) New businesses should always do a <u>break-even analysis</u> to find the break-even output.
4) It can be worked out by making a <u>break-even chart</u> — this has <u>output</u> on the <u>x-axis</u>, and <u>costs and revenues</u> on the <u>y-axis</u>.

BUSINESS EXAMPLE

Pin-Chit Ltd. make padlocks. They have fixed costs of £2000, and the variable cost per unit is £2. The selling price is £4.

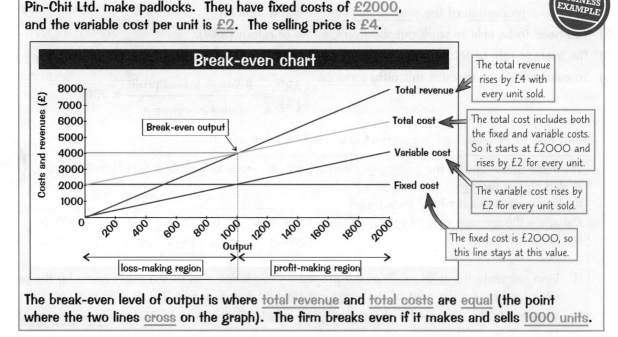

The total revenue rises by £4 with every unit sold.

The total cost includes both the fixed and variable costs. So it starts at £2000 and rises by £2 for every unit.

The variable cost rises by £2 for every unit sold.

The fixed cost is £2000, so this line stays at this value.

The break-even level of output is where total revenue and total costs are equal (the point where the two lines cross on the graph). The firm breaks even if it makes and sells 1000 units.

5) You can also use the break even analysis to see how <u>profit</u> may be affected by <u>changing output</u>. In the example above, <u>total costs</u> (and variable costs) are rising at a <u>slower rate</u> than revenue — they're rising at <u>£2</u> for every unit sold, compared to revenue rising at <u>£4</u> for every unit sold. This means that as output increases, <u>profit per unit</u> will also <u>increase</u>.

Always cover your costs — for example, sweep 'em under the rug...

Ideally, businesses would make a profit all the time, but if that's not possible then breaking even is the next best thing. Make sure you know what all the parts of a break-even chart mean — there's more on them coming up.

More on Break-Even Analysis

Even more on break-even charts here (woohoo) — this time, how to find the margin of safety for a given level of output. This is an easy way of seeing how much a business's output can fall before it starts making a loss.

You Need to be Able to Find the Margin of Safety

1) You can use a break-even chart to calculate the margin of safety.
2) The margin of safety is the gap between the current level of output and the break-even output.

- For Pin-Chit Ltd. (see previous page), if the current output is 1800 units then the margin of safety is 800 units.
- This means the firm's output will have to fall by 800 units before it starts making a loss.

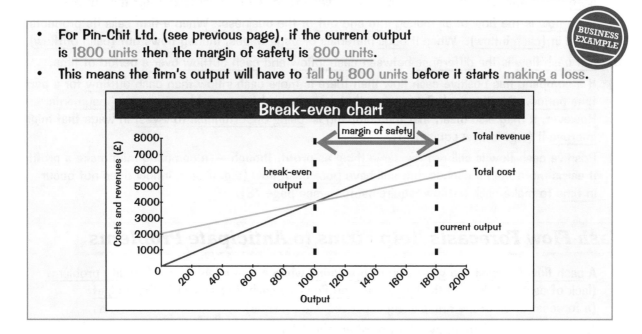

Break-Even Analysis has Advantages and Disadvantages

Advantages	Disadvantages
It's easy to work out.	It assumes that the firm can sell any quantity of the product at the current price.
It's quick. This means that if businesses decide they want to increase their margin of safety, they can take immediate action to increase sales or reduce costs to do that.	Break-even analysis assumes that all of the products are sold, without any waste.
It allows businesses to predict how changes in sales may affect costs, revenue and profits, and how changes in price and costs will affect sales.	If the data is wrong, then the results of the analysis will be wrong.
Businesses can use break-even analysis to help persuade a bank to give them a loan.	It can be complicated if it involves more than one product.
It can stop businesses from releasing products that might be difficult to sell in large quantities.	It only shows how much a business needs to sell, and not how much it actually will sell.

The margarine of safety — just use your breakfast analysis...

If you know how to read off the break-even output and the margin of safety for a given level of output, you'll be sorted for these. Don't forget to learn some advantages and disadvantages of break-even analysis too.

Cash Flow

A <u>cash flow forecast</u> shows all the money that's <u>coming into</u> and <u>going out of</u> a business.
Quite a <u>handy</u> thing for a business to know, and also GCSE Business students as it happens...

Cash is Not the Same Thing as Profit

1) <u>Cash</u> is the <u>money</u> a company can spend <u>immediately</u>, <u>profit</u> is the amount of money a company earns after <u>costs</u> have been taken into account. So a business can make a profit if it <u>earns more</u> than it <u>spends</u> but still run out of <u>cash</u> if it uses its cash to invest in other assets for the business.

2) <u>Cash flow</u> is the flow of all money <u>into</u> and <u>out of</u> the business. When a firm <u>sells</u> its products, money flows in (<u>cash inflow</u>). When it <u>buys</u> materials or <u>pays</u> wages, money flows out (<u>cash outflow</u>).

3) <u>Net cash flow</u> is the <u>difference</u> between <u>cash inflow</u> and <u>cash outflow</u> over a period of time.

4) If a company has <u>positive cash flow</u> then there is <u>more cash inflow</u> than <u>cash outflow</u> for a particular <u>time period</u>. Positive cash flow means that a company has no problem in <u>making payments</u>. However, it may also mean that the company is <u>losing opportunities</u> to <u>invest</u> in ways that might <u>improve</u> it (e.g. in new equipment).

5) Positive cash flow is still <u>not the same thing</u> as profit, though — a company may make a profit if <u>overall</u> it earns more than it spends, but still have <u>poor cash flow</u> (e.g. if cash inflow does not occur <u>in time</u> to make cash outflow requirements — see page 78).

Cash Flow Forecasts Help Firms to Anticipate Problems

1) A <u>cash flow forecast</u> is a good way of <u>predicting</u> when a firm might face a <u>liquidity problem</u> (lack of cash). It lists all the <u>inflows</u> and <u>outflows</u> of cash that appear in the <u>budget</u> (a forecast of all of the firm's likely expenses and revenue).

Businesses forecast how much they are likely to sell in a given period of time to estimate what their revenue will be — these predictions are often based on sales from previous months or years, and the firm's best guess.

2) The firm will see when an <u>overdraft</u> or other short-term finance might be needed.

3) The forecast needs to be <u>watched carefully</u> — to monitor what the impact of <u>unexpected cash flows</u> might be.

BUSINESS EXAMPLE

Cash Flow Forecast — Footy Fanzines Ltd.						
	April	May	June	July	August	Sept
Total receipts (cash inflow)	15 000	12 000	5000	5000	16 000	16 000
Total spending (cash outflow)	12 000	12 000	10 000	10 000	12 000	12 000
Net cash flow (inflow – outflow)	3000	0	(5000)	(5000)	4000	4000
Opening balance (bank balance at start of month)	1000	4000	4000	(1000)	(6000)	(2000)
Closing balance (bank balance at end of month)	4000	4000	(1000)	(6000)	(2000)	2000

Numbers in brackets are negative.

closing balance = opening balance + net cash flow

Here's an example of a <u>cash flow forecast</u> for a firm publishing football magazines.

1) In June and July, when the football season's over, the <u>net cash flow</u> is negative because more money flows <u>out</u> than <u>in</u>.

2) The firm can see it will need a source of <u>extra finance</u> to get it through from June to September.

3) It's useful to know this <u>in advance</u> because it means the firm can <u>plan</u> — it won't suddenly have to <u>panic</u> in June when it starts to <u>run out of money</u>.

I'm just a tortoise in a stupid hat, I've got nothing to do with cash flow. But I do rather think that I brighten up the page somewhat.

Cash outflow — it's just money down the drain...

Cash flow is quite easy once you've understood how the figures are worked out.
Make sure you can understand the figures in that table, and that you know why cash flow is super important.

Cash Flow — Credit

A firm's cash flow will <u>change</u> if they give their customers <u>longer to pay</u> for products — this is called <u>credit</u>.

Credit Terms Can Affect Cash Flow

<u>Credit terms</u> tell you <u>how long</u> after agreeing to buy a product the customer has to <u>pay</u>.
This can affect the <u>timings</u> of their cash flows.

1) Stuffin's Turkeys Ltd. sell most of their products in <u>December</u>.
2) This table assumes customers <u>pay when they purchase</u> the product.

Cash Flow Forecast — Stuffin's Turkeys Ltd.						
	October	November	December	January	February	March
Total receipts (cash inflow)	800	1500	12 000	300	500	300
Total payments (cash outflow)	3000	4000	2000	300	200	150
Net cash flow	(2200)	(2500)	10 000	0	300	150
Opening balance (bank balance at start of month)	3000	800	(1700)	8300	8300	8600
Closing balance (bank balance at end of month)	800	(1700)	8300	8300	8600	8750

I'm up for Turkey in December.

3) The table below assumes customers are given <u>2 months credit to pay</u>.

4) It's a bit more complicated as the <u>total receipts</u> come in <u>two months after</u> the sale is made.

Cash Flow Forecast — Stuffin's Turkeys Ltd.						
	October	November	December	January	February	March
Total sales this month (for payment in 60 days)	800	1500	12 000	300	500	300
Total receipts (cash inflow)	200	200	800	1500	12 000	300
Total payments (cash outflow)	3000	4000	2000	300	200	150
Net cash flow	(2800)	(3800)	(1200)	1200	11 800	150
Opening balance (bank balance at start of month)	3000	200	(3600)	(4800)	(3600)	8200
Closing balance (bank balance at end of month)	200	(3600)	(4800)	(3600)	8200	8350

Payment made in 2 months

> In February, the total receipts are for the turkeys bought in December. So net cash flow is 12000 − 200 = 11800

5) The main differences are:
- when customers pay immediately there is only <u>one month</u> where short-term finance is needed.
- when they pay on <u>2 month credit</u> the business will need to arrange short-term finance for <u>3 months</u>.

Me, write a naff joke? Give me a little credit please...

Make sure you know how credit terms can affect a firm's cash flow. You won't be asked to fill in a cash flow forecast in your exam, but you need to be able to look at one and work out what's going on. What fun.

Cash Flow — Problems

It's no use running from the truth. The sad fact is that a lot of firms go bust sooner or later. And poor cash flow is the most common cause of bankruptcy in businesses that are more profitable.

Poor Cash Flow Means You've Got Big Problems

1) Poor cash flow means there is not enough cash in a business to meet its day-to-day expenses — there's a lack of working capital.

2) Staff may not get paid on time — this will cause resentment and poor motivation.

3) Some suppliers offer discounts for prompt payment of invoices — the business may not be able to take advantage of these.

4) Creditors (people or firms that are owed money) may not get paid on time — they may insist on stricter credit terms in future.

5) Some creditors may not wait for payment — they might take legal action to recover the debt. If the business does not have the money it may go into receivership (a 'receiver' is appointed to reclaim money owed to the creditors by selling off the struggling firm's assets) or be forced to cease trading.

There are Three Main Reasons for Poor Cash Flow

Our new line of sandpaper beachwear hasn't sold as well as we'd hoped.

1) POOR SALES — There's a lack of demand from consumers for the firm's products, so the firm has less money coming in and it cannot pay its creditors.

2) OVERTRADING — The firm takes on too many orders — as a result it buys in too many raw materials and hires too many staff. Something goes wrong with the orders and the firm doesn't get the money from its customers quickly enough to pay its debts.

3) POOR BUSINESS DECISIONS — For example, the firm decides to bring out new products or expand into new markets but they do not bring in as much money as forecast. Bad business decisions are usually caused by not doing enough planning or market research.

There are Ways to Improve Cash Flow

1) By rescheduling payments:
   - A business could "reschedule their receipts of income". For example, they could give their customers less generous credit terms or insist they pay immediately.
   - They could try to reschedule the payments they make to their suppliers. This could include negotiating better credit terms — ideally, the credit period given to customers should be less than the credit period obtained from suppliers.

2) By reducing cash outflow. Most firms carry a stock of unsold products — they could simply sell these instead of making more.
   - By destocking, the cash inflows will be the same — but cash outflows will be reduced as less will be spent on raw materials.
   - However, eventually they'll run out of stock. At this point, they'll have to start paying out money to make more products.

3) By firms arranging to have an overdraft with their bank (see p.71).

4) By finding new sources of finance (such as a new business partner) in order to make payments.

5) By increasing cash inflow, e.g. by increasing the selling price.

Poor cash flow — best get a plumber in...

PRACTICE QUESTION

Q1 A business notices that they are unable to make certain payments on time due to poor cash flow. Suggest two actions that the business could take to make sure they make the payments on time.

Income Statements

An income statement is a type of financial statement showing how income has changed over time. Oh yeah.

There are Three Parts to an Income Statement

Here is an example of an income statement for Yummo Chocolates Ltd.

The yellow box shows the trading account, the blue box is the profit and loss account and the pink box is the appropriation account.

These figures just mean that the numbers below them are in thousands of pounds.

Income Statement
Yummo Chocolates Ltd.
Year ending 31st March 2016

	£000	£000
Revenue....................		180
Cost of sales:		
Opening stock.........	3	
Purchases..............	15	
	18	
Minus closing stock........	(5)	
Cost of sales = ...		(13)
Gross profit =.....................		167
Minus expenses		
Wages and salaries..	93	
Rent and rates........	10	
Office expenses......	28	
Advertising............	5	
Depreciation...........	8	
Other expenses.......	3	
Expenses = ...		(147)
Operating profit = ...		20
Interest payable		(2)
Profit before tax (Net profit)...		18
Taxation		(3)
Dividends		(9)
Retained profit		6

The Trading Account

1) This records the firm's gross profit or loss.

2) Revenue (or turnover) is the value of all products sold in a given period of time (see p.11).

3) Cost of sales records how much it cost to make the products sold during the year — the direct costs.

4) To find the cost of sales, first add up the value of the opening stock (the stock present at the start of the year) and the stock purchases made throughout the year. Then take away the value of the closing stock (the stock left over at the end of the year).

5) Gross profit is the difference between the revenue from selling the chocolate and the direct costs of making it. This means:

Numbers in brackets are negative.

gross profit = revenue – direct costs

The Profit and Loss Account

1) This records all the indirect costs of running the business.

2) It doesn't cover the cost of buying machinery, but it does cover depreciation — this is the amount of value which an asset has lost over a period of time due to wear and tear. Calculating depreciation allows businesses to set aside money for replacing assets.

There are two methods of calculating depreciation:

1) Straight line method. This is the easy way. If a machine costs £5000 and will wear out after about 5 years, the depreciation is simply £1000 each year.

2) Reducing balance method. This depreciates the machinery by a percentage of its value each year — a £5000 machine might depreciate by 25% each year.
   - Depreciation in year 1 = 25% of £5000 = £1250. The value is now £5000 – £1250 = £3750.
   - Depreciation in year 2 = 25% of £3750 = £938. The value is now £3750 – £938 = £2812.

3) The money left after paying all the indirect costs is called the operating profit.

4) Finally, any interest paid or received is included. What is left is true profit — net profit.

The Appropriation Account

1) The last part of the statement is only included for limited company accounts (see p.6).

2) It records where the profit has gone — to the government as tax, to shareholders as dividends, or kept in the business as retained profit.

Net profit — Wimbledon are selling off old stock...

Income statements can be a bit tricky to get the hang of. You need to add up the numbers as you go down each column to get the number on the next row. The numbers in brackets are negative, so you take them away.

Analysis — Income Statements

Now on to the good stuff — you need to be able to analyse financial statements. That means being able to say how well a business is doing, and how it might improve from the info in the statements. In real life this analysis helps companies make business decisions. First up, the income statement — make sure you can analyse one on its own, and compare it with statements from previous years.

Values on the Income Statement Show Business Performance

1) Gross profit — If gross profit is low, managers need to look at ways of reducing the cost of making the product, or increasing the revenue, to make gross profit higher.

2) Operating profit — If this is significantly lower than gross profit, it could show that the company's operating expenses are a weak area, e.g. it may invest a lot of money in people or buildings. Management could take steps to reduce these expenses. Banks and investors will look at this figure to assess the risk of lending to or investing in the business. If the operating profit is too low then they may be too worried about losing their money to make an investment.

3) Retained profit tells you if the company is profitable or not — shareholders and potential investors will look at this figure to assess investments. It also shows how much internal finance the company has available to invest, and so what potential it has to get bigger.

Income Statements from Separate Years Can be Compared

The income statements from two consecutive years for a yacht-building firm are shown below. You can analyse each individually to see how well the business has done in one year, or compare business performance between both years:

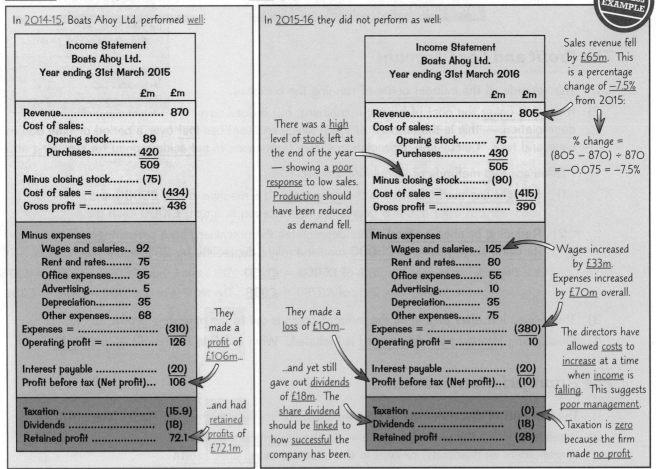

In 2014-15, Boats Ahoy Ltd. performed well:

Income Statement
Boats Ahoy Ltd.
Year ending 31st March 2015

	£m	£m
Revenue		870
Cost of sales:		
Opening stock	89	
Purchases	420	
	509	
Minus closing stock	(75)	
Cost of sales =		(434)
Gross profit =		436
Minus expenses		
Wages and salaries	92	
Rent and rates	75	
Office expenses	35	
Advertising	5	
Depreciation	35	
Other expenses	68	
Expenses =		(310)
Operating profit =		126
Interest payable		(20)
Profit before tax (Net profit)...		106
Taxation		(15.9)
Dividends		(18)
Retained profit		72.1

They made a profit of £106m...

...and had retained profits of £72.1m.

In 2015-16 they did not perform as well:

Income Statement
Boats Ahoy Ltd.
Year ending 31st March 2016

	£m	£m
Revenue		805
Cost of sales:		
Opening stock	75	
Purchases	430	
	505	
Minus closing stock	(90)	
Cost of sales =		(415)
Gross profit =		390
Minus expenses		
Wages and salaries	125	
Rent and rates	80	
Office expenses	55	
Advertising	10	
Depreciation	35	
Other expenses	75	
Expenses =		(380)
Operating profit =		10
Interest payable		(20)
Profit before tax (Net profit)...		(10)
Taxation		(0)
Dividends		(18)
Retained profit		(28)

There was a high level of stock left at the end of the year — showing a poor response to low sales. Production should have been reduced as demand fell.

They made a loss of £10m...

...and yet still gave out dividends of £18m. The share dividend should be linked to how successful the company has been.

Sales revenue fell by £65m. This is a percentage change of −7.5% from 2015:

% change = (805 − 870) ÷ 870 = −0.075 = −7.5%

Wages increased by £33m. Expenses increased by £70m overall.

The directors have allowed costs to increase at a time when income is falling. This suggests poor management.

Taxation is zero because the firm made no profit.

Business performance — it ain't no song and dance...

There's quite a bit to get your head around here, so make sure you're comfortable with this stuff before moving on. And have a look back at the previous page if you need to remind yourself what these pesky money terms mean.

Profit Margins

Just to throw some more numbers into the book, here's a page on profit margins.
They show what happens to each pound spent by a customer, and there are two types...

Gross Profit Margin Ignores Indirect Costs

Gross profit margin is the fraction of every pound spent by customers
that doesn't go directly towards making a product:

> Gross profit margin = gross profit ÷ sales (revenue) × 100

Here's how to calculate the gross profit margin using the income statement on page 79:

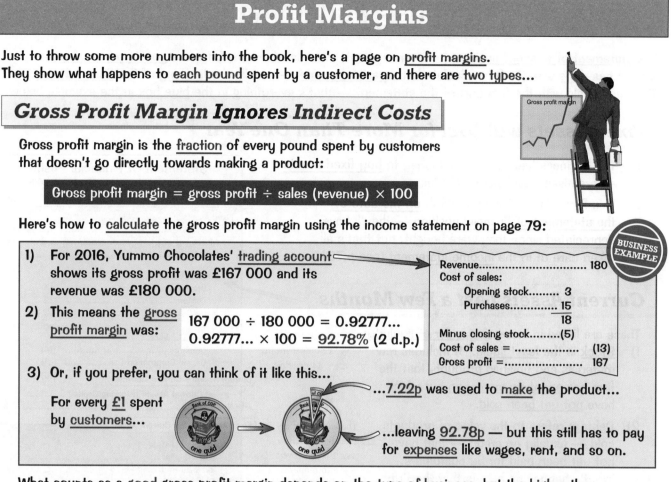

1) For 2016, Yummo Chocolates' trading account shows its gross profit was £167 000 and its revenue was £180 000.

Revenue	180
Cost of sales:	
Opening stock	3
Purchases	15
	18
Minus closing stock	(5)
Cost of sales =	(13)
Gross profit =	167

2) This means the gross profit margin was:

167 000 ÷ 180 000 = 0.92777...
0.92777... × 100 = 92.78% (2 d.p.)

3) Or, if you prefer, you can think of it like this...

For every £1 spent by customers...

...7.22p was used to make the product...

...leaving 92.78p — but this still has to pay for expenses like wages, rent, and so on.

What counts as a good gross profit margin depends on the type of business, but the higher the
percentage the better. The margin can be improved by increasing prices or reducing the direct
cost of sales. Some businesses (e.g. a supermarket chain) can have a low gross profit margin
because they sell in high volumes and they need to keep their prices competitive to survive.

Net Profit Margin Takes All Costs into Account

Net profit margin is the fraction of every pound spent by customers that the company gets to keep
(after all its costs have been paid):

> Net profit margin = net profit ÷ sales (revenue) × 100

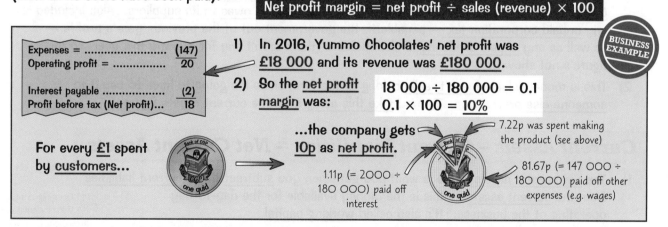

Expenses =	(147)
Operating profit =	20
Interest payable	(2)
Profit before tax (Net profit)...	18

1) In 2016, Yummo Chocolates' net profit was £18 000 and its revenue was £180 000.

2) So the net profit margin was:

18 000 ÷ 180 000 = 0.1
0.1 × 100 = 10%

For every £1 spent by customers...

...the company gets 10p as net profit.

1.11p (= 2000 ÷ 180 000) paid off interest

7.22p was spent making the product (see above)

81.67p (= 147 000 ÷ 180 000) paid off other expenses (e.g. wages)

Just like for gross profit margins, what counts as a good net profit margin depends on the business,
but the higher it is, the better. Net profit margin is often larger for new companies which are still small and
don't have many indirect costs. As businesses grow, these costs go up and net profit margin decreases.

Gross profit — it's a disgusting amount of money...

PRACTICE QUESTION

Q1 A business makes £200 000 in revenue in one year. At the beginning of the year it has stock worth
£15 000 and it makes purchases worth £45 000 throughout the year. At the end of the year it has
closing stock worth £20 000. Calculate the business's gross profit margin.

Statements of Financial Position

The <u>statement of financial position</u> (or balance sheet) records where the business <u>got its money from</u>, and what it has <u>done</u> with it. It is calculated at a <u>particular date</u> — usually the <u>last day</u> of the <u>financial year</u>. This page deals with the first part of the statement — that's everything in the <u>blue box</u> in the example below.

Fixed Assets will Last for More Than One Year

1) The business has used some money to <u>buy fixed assets</u> — premises, machinery, vehicles.

2) This figure is what they're worth <u>on the date of the statement of financial position</u> — they'll have <u>depreciated</u> since they were bought, but that's all taken care of in the <u>income statement</u> (see p.79).

Current Assets Last a Few Months

These are listed in increasing <u>order of liquidity</u>:

1) <u>Stock</u> is the <u>least liquid</u>. It includes raw materials and finished products that the firm has <u>spent its money on</u> but which have <u>not yet been sold</u>.

2) <u>Debtors</u> refers to the value of <u>products sold</u> — usually on credit — that have <u>not yet been paid for</u> by customers. What's happening here is that the firm is <u>lending its money</u> to customers so they can buy its products.

3) <u>Cash</u> is the most liquid. This is money the firm <u>hasn't spent</u> on anything yet — it's just <u>sitting in the bank</u>.

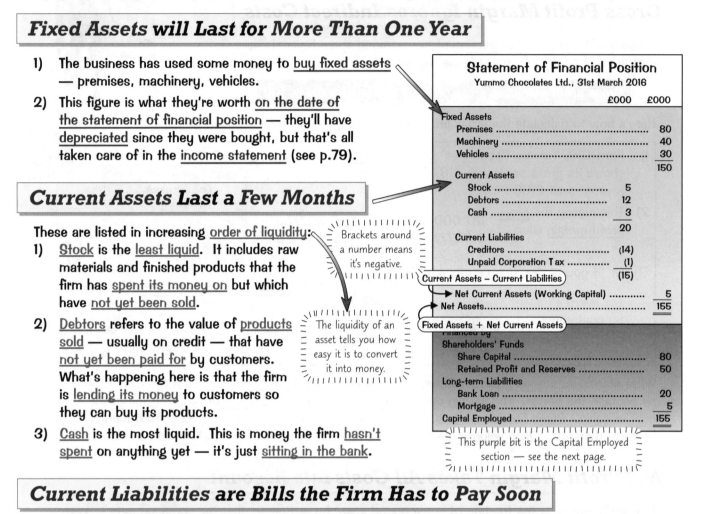

Brackets around a number means it's negative.

The liquidity of an asset tells you how easy it is to convert it into money.

Statement of Financial Position
Yummo Chocolates Ltd., 31st March 2016

	£000	£000
Fixed Assets		
Premises		80
Machinery		40
Vehicles		30
		150
Current Assets		
Stock	5	
Debtors	12	
Cash	3	
	20	
Current Liabilities		
Creditors	(14)	
Unpaid Corporation Tax	(1)	
Current Assets – Current Liabilities	(15)	
Net Current Assets (Working Capital)		5
Net Assets		155
Fixed Assets + Net Current Assets		
Financed by		
Shareholders' Funds		
Share Capital		80
Retained Profit and Reserves		50
Long-term Liabilities		
Bank Loan		20
Mortgage		5
Capital Employed		155

This purple bit is the Capital Employed section — see the next page.

Current Liabilities are Bills the Firm Has to Pay Soon

1) These are any payments the firm will have to make <u>within one year</u> of the date on the balance sheet. <u>Creditors</u> is the opposite of debtors — it is money the <u>firm owes</u> to its <u>suppliers</u>. Also included is any <u>unpaid corporation tax</u> — payable to the government out of the previous year's profits — as well as any <u>unpaid dividends</u> to shareholders (there aren't any for Yummo this year, so this figure's not shown).

2) This is money which <u>doesn't really</u> belong to the firm, since it's going to have to pay it to <u>someone else</u> pretty soon. So you <u>take this away</u> from the current assets figure...

Current Assets – Current Liabilities = Net Current Assets

1) The <u>net current assets</u> figure is what you get when you <u>subtract</u> those <u>current liabilities</u> from the <u>current assets</u> — this is the money available for the day-to-day operating of the business. It's also called <u>working capital</u>.

2) Add the <u>net current assets</u> to the <u>fixed assets</u> and you get the <u>net assets</u>, or net worth, of the business. This is the amount the firm would make if it <u>sold</u> all its assets (in theory) — it's what the firm is <u>worth</u>.

Both these calculations are labelled on the statement of financial position above.

Current assets — I'm more of a sultana girl myself...

You're going to finish this off on the next page — but try to make sure you've understood everything so far. Make sure you know the names of all the headings on the statement of financial position and what they all mean. Also give yourself a quick test on what the difference is between assets and liabilities. Not much, eh...?

More on Statements of Financial Position

Now for the second part of the statement of financial position — where all the <u>money came from</u> to <u>create</u> the net worth of the business. Originally it came from <u>shareholders</u> buying the shares, and money <u>loaned to it</u> by other people — over the years <u>retained profit</u> will be added to this, and possibly <u>more loans</u>. Nifty.

Shareholders' Funds Came from the Firm's Owners

Shareholders' funds include <u>share capital</u> and <u>retained profit and reserves</u> on the statement:

Share Capital

- This is the money put into the business when shares were <u>originally issued</u>. This might have been years and years ago for <u>long-established</u> companies.
- This is not the same as what the shares are <u>currently worth</u>. Most shares traded on the stock exchange are <u>second-hand</u> — the person selling them gets the cash, not the firm.
- Firms can raise <u>new capital</u> by issuing <u>new shares</u> (see p.72). The usual way is to have a <u>rights issue</u>. This is where existing shareholders are offered new shares at a <u>reduced price</u>.

This is the Capital Employed section from Yummo Chocolates' statement of financial position (see previous page).

```
Financed by
Shareholders' Funds
    Share Capital .......................    80
    Retained Profit and Reserves ......    50
Long-term Liabilities
    Bank Loan .........................    20
    Mortgage ..........................     5
Capital Employed ......................   155
```

Shareholders' funds + Long-term liabilities

Retained profit and reserves

- This shows all the <u>profit</u> that the firm has made over the years that it has decided to <u>keep</u> instead of paying in dividends.
- Firms retain profit to finance <u>future investment</u> or to protect the firm against <u>future problems</u>.
- This comes under "shareholders' funds" because profits are really the <u>shareholders' money</u> — they've just decided to <u>leave it in the firm</u> rather than taking it out as dividends.

Long-term Liabilities — Money Owed to Others

See pages 71-72 for more on sources of finance.

1) Firms don't just get money from their shareholders — they <u>borrow it</u> from other people as well. Included here are any debts that will take <u>more than one year</u> to repay, e.g. <u>bank loans</u>.

2) Debts payable in <u>less than a year</u> come under <u>current liabilities</u> instead — see the previous page. It's all money the company owes, but it's <u>conventional</u> to <u>split it up</u> like that.

Capital Employed is the Total Put into the Business

1) Capital employed is what you get when you <u>add</u> shareholders' funds to long-term liabilities. This is <u>equal to net assets</u> (see previous page) because it shows where the money to fund them came from.

2) If you're <u>confused</u>, think about it this way — all the money the business <u>has got</u> (from shareholders and borrowing from other people) is accounted for by <u>capital employed</u>. And everything it's <u>done with the money</u> it got (bought premises, kept it as cash, etc.) is listed under <u>net assets</u>. They have to be the <u>same</u> — because money <u>doesn't just vanish</u>.

Share capital — but I want to keep it all for myself...

Q1 A business has long-term liabilities of £4m and shareholders' funds of £6m.
   a) How much capital is employed in the business?
   b) £2m of the shareholders' funds is from retained profit. What is meant by retained profit?

Analysis — Statements of Financial Position

As well as income statements (see p.79-80), you need to be able to analyse statements of financial position (sorry...). Doing this can help a company see how it's performing, and make decisions about the business.

Statements of Financial Position Show a Snapshot in Time...

1) The statement of financial position can be used to assess a business's performance at a point in time.

2) It shows the sources of capital for the business (see pages 71-72).
Long-term loans and mortgages are better sources than overdrafts, since they are less expensive.

3) It can also be used to work out the working capital and liquidity of the business, which can be useful in making business decisions. E.g. if the business has a large amount of working capital, they could invest this money in new equipment or use it to pay off some loans.

See p.82 for how to find the working capital and liquidity of a business from its statement of financial position.

...and Can be Used to Show Trends Over Time

1) Statements of financial position can also be compared across several consecutive years.

2) Here are some examples of pieces of information that can be compared and what they can tell you:

- Fixed assets — A quick increase in this indicates that the company has invested, e.g. in property or machinery. As a result, this means that the company's profit may increase in the future.

- Retained profits or reserves — Increases in this suggest an increase in profits.

- Liabilities — The amount and type of liabilities can indicate how well-managed a business is. A company with a high value of loan capital and a relatively low value of share capital or reserves would be in trouble if interest rates went up. If long-term liabilities have increased, the business might reduce its borrowing in the future.

For a reminder of these terms, flick back to pages 82-83.

3) This comparison can be used to make business decisions. For example, if a business shows slow growth by not having more assets year on year, the company may decide to reduce dividends and retain more of their profit to invest in the business.

Several Stakeholders Will be Interested in a Financial Analysis

1) Stakeholders (see p.10) can use the financial analysis of the income statement or the statement of financial position to check how healthy the business is. E.g. growing net assets may indicate that the business is healthy, whereas low net assets may indicate that the business is borrowing too much.

2) Here are some examples of possible stakeholders and other ways they might use a financial analysis:

- Existing shareholders — these are entitled to a share of the profits (the share dividend). They may use the income statement to assess the performance of the directors of the business, to see if they have made sensible decisions (e.g. reducing expenses when revenue falls).

- Potential shareholders or lenders — these may look at how much profit the business makes. If the business makes enough profit, they may consider investing in it or lending it money.

- Employees — these will be interested in whether the company makes a profit or a loss. A profitable business will be able to afford to give employees a pay rise, but a loss-making business might make some workers redundant.

- The government — the government receives corporation tax from the business. It uses the income statement to calculate how much tax the business needs to pay.

- Suppliers — these are likely to be interested in the liquidity of a business — the more liquid it is, the better it will be at paying bills, so they will be more likely to sell it goods.

Tongs and spatulas — some other steakholders to remember...

I reckon this page makes it a little bit easier to see how a statement of financial position can show how a business is doing. Cover the page and scribble down all the people who might be interested in this information.

Analysis — Competitors

Businesses can compare their data with data from similar businesses. This allows them to assess their performance against their competitors and find places where they could improve. Real handy stuff...

You Can Compare Financial Statements from Competitors

1) The income statement can be used to compare different businesses' revenue, expenses and profit.

2) The statement of financial position can be used to compare how much each business is worth and how much they have in liabilities.

3) It can be difficult to directly compare certain aspects of the financial statements, because the competitors may work in different ways and have very different figures. One way of directly comparing how well businesses are doing is to calculate gross and net profit margins (see p.81).

4) Here is a comparison of the performance of two perfume companies in 2015-16:

Trendy Scents Plc

Income Statement
Trendy Scents Plc
Year ending 31 March 2016

	£m	£m
Revenue		1203
Minus cost of sales		
Opening stock	130	
Purchases	506	
	636	
Minus closing stock	(98)	
		(538)
Gross profit		665
Minus expenses		
Wages and salaries	112	
Rent and rates	102	
Office expenses	42	
Advertising	45	
Depreciation	33	
Other expenses	68	
		(402)
Operating profit		263
Interest payable		(13)
Profit before taxation (net profit)		250
Taxation		(50)
Dividends		(115)
Retained profit		85

1) Trendy Scents Plc had a higher revenue than Naturo Pong Plc.

2) But Trendy Scents Plc also had a higher cost of sales and higher expenses. For example, Trendy Scents Plc spent much more on advertising than Naturo Pong Plc.

3) However, to be able to compare the values in the statements directly, you have to calculate their gross and net profit margins:

	Trendy Scents Plc	Naturo Pong Plc
Gross Profit Margin	55%	44%
Net Profit Margin	21%	1.9%

Naturo Pong Plc has a very low net profit margin. This would be worrying to the company managers as it suggests that a reduction in revenue in the future could lead to a loss rather than a profit. Trendy Scents Plc has a healthier gross and net profit margin.

Naturo Pong Plc

BUSINESS EXAMPLE

Income Statement
Naturo Pong Plc
Year ending 31 March 2016

	£m	£m
Revenue		780
Minus cost of sales		
Opening stock	89	
Purchases	420	
	509	
Minus closing stock	(75)	
		(434)
Gross profit		346
Minus expenses		
Wages and salaries	93	
Rent and rates	75	
Office expenses	35	
Advertising	5	
Depreciation	35	
Other expenses	68	
		(311)
Operating profit		35
Interest payable		(20)
Profit before taxation (net profit)		15
Taxation		(2)
Dividends		(9)
Retained profit		4

Statement of Financial Position
Trendy Scents Plc, 31 March 2016

	£m	£m
Fixed Assets		
Premises		670
Machinery		275
Vehicles		10
		955
Current Assets		
Stock	103	
Debtors	75	
Cash	45	
	223	
Current Liabilities		
Creditors	(110)	
Unpaid Corporation Tax	(60)	
	(170)	
Net Current Assets (Working Capital)		53
Net Assets		1008
Financed by		
Shareholders' Funds		
Share Capital		456
Retained Profit and Reserves		150
Long-term Liabilities		
Bank Loan		395
Mortgage		7
Capital Employed		1008

4) The statement of financial position also shows differences between the two companies.

5) Trendy Scents Plc has more fixed and current assets than Naturo Pong Plc. This may mean that it will be better able to cover its costs in the future.

6) However, Trendy Scents Plc also has larger long-term liabilities, including a larger bank loan, than Naturo Pong Plc. This means that it will have to pay more money out over time, to cover these costs.

Statement of Financial Position
Naturo Pong Plc, 31 March 2016

	£m	£m
Fixed Assets		
Premises		550
Machinery		250
Vehicles		6
		806
Current Assets		
Stock	75	
Debtors	45	
Cash	12	
	132	
Current Liabilities		
Creditors	(62)	
Unpaid Corporation Tax	(10)	
	(72)	
Net Current Assets (Working Capital)		60
Net Assets		866
Financed by		
Shareholders' Funds		
Share Capital		560
Retained Profit and Reserves		146
Long-term Liabilities		
Bank Loan		154
Mortgage		6
Capital Employed		866

Good column technique, excellent profit calculations — I give it 10/10

Wait, it gets better — you can also use both types of statements together. E.g. you can compare whether the liabilities have increased faster than sales. Make sure you can think of how to interpret each bit of both statements.

Case Study — Finance

Now it's time to put the theory into action. The case study below shows the income statements for a company in <u>two consecutive years</u>. Have a <u>quick look</u> through both and then try out the <u>questions</u>.

Business Report: Finance

Goat Courture Plc

The table on the right shows the income statements for two consecutive years for a pet fashion and accessories company — Goat Couture Plc.

		2014-15		2015-16	
		£	£	£	£
Revenue			129000		113000
Cost of sales					
	Opening stock	20055		13875	
	Purchases	45679		93233	
	Minus closing stock	(13875)		(19201)	
Cost of sales			(51859)		(87907)
Gross profit			77141		25093
Minus expenses					
	Wages and salaries	51000		42000	
	Rent and rates	3400		3400	
	Office expenses	890		770	
	Advertising	2360		1346	
	Depreciation	1400		1300	
	Other	64		52	
Expenses			(59114)		(48868)
Operating profit			18027		(23775)
Interest payable			(560)		(410)
Profit before tax (net profit)			17467		(24185)
Taxation			(1580)		0
Dividends			(2300)		(400)
Retained profit			?		(24585)

Case Study Questions

The following questions should help you to analyse the income statements above. Take your time and make sure you read the question. You can also flick back to previous pages if you need a bit of help.

1) Calculate the retained profit for the company in 2014-15.

2) Calculate the net profit margin for Goat Couture Plc in 2014-15.
   Give your answer to 3 significant figures.

3) Calculate the percentage change in revenue between the two financial years.
   Give your answer to 3 significant figures.

4) Suggest why the company made a loss in 2015-16.

5) Apart from comparing income statements from consecutive years,
   suggest what else the company could do to analyse its performance.

Too many numbers... my brain... it... hurts...

Well, I hope that you've got the idea of how to compare income statements. Don't forget that you might get similar questions on a statement of financial position instead, so make sure you're comfortable analysing them too.

Revision Summary

This section's pretty tricky, so make sure you've got your head around all of the financial <u>terminology</u>, not to mention both the <u>income statement</u> and the <u>statement of financial position</u>, before doing these questions.

1) Give one difference between a government grant and a loan.

2) Give one disadvantage of using an overdraft compared to other forms of borrowing.

3) Describe what is meant by a hire purchase.

4) Give one disadvantage of using fixed assets to raise finance.

5) Give one advantage of using internal sources of finance, over external sources of finance.

6) Give one factor that may affect the source of finance used by a company.

7) Give one reason why a business might invest money in new premises.

8) Write the equation for finding the average rate of return for an investment.

9) Give the two different types of costs that a business may record.

10) What is the break-even output?

11) *Find the break-even output on the break-even chart below.

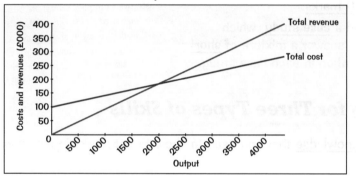

12) What is the margin of safety on a break-even chart?

13) Give one disadvantage of using break-even analysis.

14) What is meant by net cash flow?

15) How do you calculate the closing balance for a period on a cash flow forecast?

16) Describe how credit can affect cash flow for a business.

17) Give one reason why poor cash flow can make running a business difficult.

18) Describe one reason why a business may have poor cash flow.

19) How is gross profit calculated on an income statement?

20) Give two pieces of information that are within the profit and loss account of an income statement.

21) Give two pieces of information on an income statement that can be used to analyse a business's performance.

22) a) What does the net profit margin represent?
    b) How is the net profit margin calculated?

23) What are meant by fixed assets?

24) Is cash more or less liquid than stock?

25) How is the worth of a firm calculated?

26) Describe what is meant by share capital.

27) What would a rapid increase in the value of fixed assets on a statement of financial position indicate to potential investors?

28) Give one stakeholder that would be interested in the performance of a business and explain why they would be interested.

29) Give one reason why it may be difficult to directly compare financial statements from two competitors.

* Answer to q11: the break-even output is 2000 units.

The Exams

By now your brain should be full of Business knowledge, ready to <u>impress</u> the examiners. These pages have info and tips on <u>what to expect</u> in the exams, so that you can <u>ace them</u>.

There Are Two Exam Papers — Paper 1 and Paper 2

Paper 1

- Paper 1 is <u>1 hour and 45 minutes</u> long.
- It's worth <u>90 marks</u> and is <u>50%</u> of your total Business GCSE.
- It'll test you on information from Sections <u>1</u>, <u>2</u>, <u>3</u> and <u>4</u> of this book.

Paper 2

- Paper 2 is <u>1 hour and 45 minutes</u> long.
- It's worth <u>90 marks</u> and is <u>50%</u> of your total Business GCSE.
- It'll test you on information from Sections <u>1</u>, <u>2</u>, <u>5</u> and <u>6</u> of this book.

1) In both papers there'll be <u>three</u> sections.
2) <u>Section A</u> is a mixture of <u>multiple choice</u> and <u>short answer</u> questions, and is worth <u>20 marks</u>.
3) <u>Sections B</u> and <u>C</u> are both based around a <u>case study</u>, which could include some <u>data</u>. You'll have to answer a mixture of <u>short</u> and <u>long questions</u> related to the information in each case study.

> At the end of each section in this book, you'll find a case study followed by some questions. These case studies may be illustrative examples, or real-life businesses. You don't need to learn the details of these case studies, but you should have a go at answering the questions to help you with Sections B and C in the exams.

The Examiners are Looking for Three Types of Skills

There are basically three types of <u>skill</u> and <u>knowledge</u> that you need to show to get marks in the exams:

Demonstrate knowledge and understanding

- This skill is all about... well... <u>recalling</u>, <u>selecting</u> and <u>communicating</u>.
- You need to show that you've got a really good <u>understanding</u> of the facts, and that you can use appropriate <u>business terms</u>, e.g. sole trader, marketing mix, supply chain.

Apply knowledge and understanding

- This skill is all about <u>applying</u> what you know to different situations.
- Make sure your answer is <u>relevant</u> to the situation that's been described.
- For example, an exam question might tell you about a <u>sole trader</u> who wants to buy a new piece of equipment, and ask you to suggest how they could raise the necessary finance. Here, you wouldn't want to suggest that the company issue more shares (since only a <u>limited company</u> can have shares and sole traders are <u>unlimited</u>).

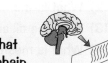

Analyse and evaluate to demonstrate understanding, make judgements and draw conclusions

- This skill is all about using <u>evidence</u> to make <u>judgements</u> and reach <u>conclusions</u>.
- For example, if you recommend that a business raise money using a mortgage rather than an overdraft, you need to explain <u>why</u>, using what you know about finance.
- Your ideas need to be <u>structured</u> in a logical way so that your arguments make <u>sense</u>.
- Often, these questions won't have a <u>right</u> answer. The important thing is using <u>evidence</u> from the question to <u>support</u> the conclusion you've come to.

Brown, leather and slightly battered — a typical briefcase study...

So, two exams, 1 hour and 45 minutes each. Simple. Well... maybe 'simple' is a bit strong — they don't give these GCSEs away. But knowing what to expect when you go into your exam can make your life that little bit easier.

Answering Questions

Doing well in Business is made a whole heap easier if you know what the examiners are looking for.

Make Sure you Read the Question

1) Command words are just the bit of the question that tell you what to do.

2) You'll find answering exam questions much easier if you understand exactly what they mean, so here's a summary of the most common command words:

Command word	What to do
State or identify	These words ask for a statement — you don't need to back it up with evidence.
Explain	This means you need to give reasons for things. You need to show that you understand the connection between things that happen in the world and the effects they have on businesses.
Analyse	This means "Examine in detail." You should talk about the main features of the thing you're analysing. Then explain how or why these features work together to lead to the end result.
Calculate	Some questions ask for a bit of maths. Remember to show your working.
Complete	You need to fill in the missing parts of some information you've been given (e.g. complete a table).
Recommend	You'll be given some information about a business and asked to say whether the business should do something, or to choose between two options for what the business could do.
Evaluate	You should discuss both sides of an issue. You should finish your answer with a conclusion giving an overall judgement.
Give reasons for your answer	This means you need to include lots of points and explain why they're relevant to your answer. Link your ideas together to build a balanced argument.
Use evidence to support your answer	This means you need to pick out specific information from a case study or piece of data that you've been given, in order to back up your answer.

3) In general, you'll need to spend more time and write more for questions that are worth more marks.

4) Questions asking you to analyse a situation or recommend a decision for a business to make are worth the most — they'll be 6, 9 or 12 marks. For these questions, it might help to write a quick plan to make sure you don't miss anything, and to make sure you show all the skills from the previous page.

You'll have to Answer Questions About Case Studies

1) For questions that are based on case study information or on data, make sure you use evidence from the case study or data set as well as your knowledge of Business in your answer.

2) For questions using 'analyse' or 'recommend' command words, there will usually be advantages and disadvantages of a situation to think about — to get all the marks, you'll need to give both sides of the argument before coming to a conclusion.

You'll often have to consider how different parts of a business work together when answering case study questions.

3) Before you get started on your answer, read the case study and any data all the way through. Then read the whole question carefully and make sure you've understood what you're being asked to do.

You'll be Tested on Your Maths Skills

1) Maths is everywhere, and your GCSE Business exams are no exception.

2) You might be asked do some calculations using financial data, or interpret a graph.

3) If you're doing a calculation question, make sure you show your working — even if your final answer's wrong, you could still get some marks if your method was correct.

4) And don't forget to take a calculator to the exams.

Sick of revision yet? Give reasons for your answer...

For each question in the exam, look at the command words and the number of marks. Remember that longer questions are usually testing your judgement as well as your knowledge, so support your ideas with evidence.

Answers

Note on Answers:
A lot of the time in Business, there isn't really a "right answer". Instead, it's about being able to explain yourself and justify your decisions.

Section 1 — Business in the Real World

Page 5 — Business Ownership Structures
Q1 E.g. having her brother as a partner means he could put capital into the business, meaning it could grow faster. However, Jennifer would have to share the profits of the business with her brother, so she could end up with less money for herself.

Page 9 — More on Business Objectives
Q1 a) E.g. Green Machines could set a profit target for the year. At the end of the year it could compare its actual profits with the target and see whether it has reached the target.

b) E.g. it might focus more on customer satisfaction rather than maximising profits in order to persuade customers to buy lawnmowers from them, rather than from their competitors.

Page 11 — Revenue, Costs and Profit
Q1 a) average unit cost = total cost ÷ output
= 12 500 ÷ 5000 = **£2.50**

b) revenue = sales × price = 5000 × 7 = £35 000
profit = revenue − costs = 35 000 − 12 500
= **£22 500**

Page 14 — Expanding Businesses
Q1 a) E.g. the law of increased dimensions means that, even though the factory is double the size, it doesn't cost twice as much to operate it. This means that the average unit cost of producing each board game will fall.

b) Expanding will lead to economies of scale, meaning that the average unit cost will fall. This means that Lucky Dice can afford to charge less for their games and still make a profit.

c) Hint — you should state one diseconomy of scale that Lucky Dice might experience, and explain how it will affect the business.
E.g. Lucky Dice have hired more staff. Having more staff means it will be harder to communicate within the company. This could cause the employees to become demotivated and productivity to go down.

Page 17 — Case Study — Business in the Real World
Q1 tertiary sector

Q2 E.g. as the business grows, there will be more risks, and having limited liability means that Sophie will only lose the amount of money she invested if the business closes down with large debts.

Q3 Hint — for each risk and benefit you choose, make sure you explain how it will affect Scoop of the Day.
E.g. expanding the business means that Scoop of the Day will benefit from economies of scale. For example, it will be buying ice cream and other supplies in larger quantities, so may be able to get them at a cheaper unit price than before. However, opening a new store means the business will have more costs than before. For example, Sophie will need to pay extra staff to run the new shop and also pay for the extra rent. This could be risky if Sophie hasn't checked that the business will be able to afford these extra expenses.

Q4 Hint — for whichever site you choose, you need to justify why this site would be better than the other two using information from the case study. Make sure you discuss the effects of factors such as cost, location of the market and competition.

E.g. Sophie should choose 12 Market Street. This is a popular area, so the market is likely to be larger than Sutcliff Park and a similar size to Mega Mall. Even though 12 Market Street is more expensive than Sutcliff Park, having a larger market means that the café should sell more, which should cover the extra cost. There is some competition on the street from other cafés, but none of these cafés sell ice cream, so Sophie will still have a unique selling point. At Mega Mall, the shop would be surrounded by other food outlets. This could be good, as people will come to the area for food, but the competition also means some of these people will use the other cafés. At the park, there is no competition in the winter, but during the summer an ice cream van will be in direct competition with the café. As summer is likely to be the busiest period for the café, it could have a big impact on Sophie's sales. Finally, the café Sophie originally set up was in a similar site to 12 Market Street. Sophie has already shown that this type of location is a success, as shown by her increasing yearly profits. So setting up a second shop in a similar type of location should also be a success.

Section 2 — Influences on Business

Page 20 — Consumer Law
Q1 E.g. the product is not fit for purpose as it can't be used to store normal pens / the product doesn't match its description, which said it was suitable for standard stationery needs.

Page 24 — Unemployment and Consumer Spending
Q1 Hint: for both part a) and b), you need to explain the effect on the business, not just describe what might happen.

a) E.g. George is likely to see an increase in sales. This is because people will be spending a smaller proportion of their income on needs than before, so they'll have more to spend on wants such as eating at restaurants. This means demand for George's restaurant is likely to go up.

b) E.g. George's sales are likely to go down. This is because people will be spending more of their income on needs than before, so they'll have less to spend on wants such as dining out at restaurants. So demand for George's restaurant is likely to go down.

Page 26 — Competition
Q1 a) E.g. high competition because there's likely to be lots of shops selling clothes on a local high street.

b) E.g. low competition because not very many people own reptiles, and not many will take them to a reptile groomer, so the market won't be big enough to support many businesses.

c) E.g. no competition because the hay fever treatment is a new development, so there won't be any competition until other businesses start selling similar products.

Page 30 — Case Study — Influences on Business
Q1 Hint: for each thing you choose, make sure you explain why it may give Aldi a competitive advantage.
E.g. Aldi provides goods at lower prices than other supermarkets, which will encourage customers to go to Aldi as they should spend less money. Aldi also has a policy to not send waste from its stores to landfill. This could encourage customers to shop at Aldi if they want to buy goods from a shop that is trying to reduce its impact on the environment.

Q2 E.g. the graph shows that between 2008/9 and 2013/14, median disposable income was lower than it had been in 2007/8. This means it's likely that more consumers will have been trying to save money during this period. As Aldi provides products at lower prices than other supermarkets, consumers looking to save money are likely to have started shopping at Aldi, leading to its market share going up.

Q3 a) E.g. in February 2016, Aldi was already paying staff at least £8.40 per hour, which is above the level of the National Living Wage. So it wouldn't have had to increase staff members' wages to follow the new law, and profits are unlikely to have been affected.

b) E.g. Aldi gets lots of its produce from British suppliers. This means that the cost of this produce is less likely to be affected by a fall in the value of the pound compared to if it was supplied from abroad. So profits are unlikely to be affected a huge amount, though they might go down slightly if produce from abroad becomes more expensive and they don't raise prices.

Section 3 — Business Operations

Page 33 — More on Supply Chains
Q1 a) E.g. supplies could arrive more quickly if they came from within the UK, meaning there would be less impact on production if supplies arrived damaged and had to be replaced. / It would cost less to transport supplies if they came from within the UK.

b) E.g. the new arrangement may mean that the company is able to get a better price and value for the wicks, which will lower its costs. / It may be able to establish a better relationship with its suppliers and therefore make sure that processes are being carried out efficiently and cost-effectively. / Its new arrangement may mean that it only orders the supplies that it needs, so it will reduce waste.

Page 34 — Methods of Production
Q1 a) job production

b) E.g. products made by job production are expensive so the theatre company may not have been able to afford to have all of the costumes made by Which Stitch. Job production can take a long time so there may not have been enough time for Which Stitch to make all of the costumes before the pantomime.

Page 37 — Quality Management
Q1 E.g. they could monitor how many customer complaints they get about the events they organise. They could carry out customer surveys to find out how satisfied customers are with the quality of the events they organise.

Page 40 — Case Study — Business Operations
Q1 E.g. Marks and Spencer works very closely with its suppliers. This helps to ensure that processes are being carried out in ways that are most efficient and cost-effective, which helps to keep the business running smoothly and prevent money from being wasted. / Marks and Spencer ensure that the factories that supply them meet their minimum quality standards. This helps to ensure that Marks and Spencer continues to sell high quality goods, so its reputation for quality remains high.

Q2 Workers put their names on the batch cards. If any problems with the quality of the products are introduced during their part of the process, they will be held responsible. This helps to encourage workers to think about the quality of their work, which is the aim of a total quality management strategy.

Q3 The recall of products could have negatively affected Marks and Spencer's image and reputation, which could have meant new and existing customers were put off buying products from the business.

Q4 Hint — you should identify at least three examples from the case study of how Marks and Spencer provide customer service and explain why each one is good for the customer. Remember to talk about how advances in technology have helped too.
E.g. Marks and Spencer responded to the views of customers and stopped playing music in its stores. This made the shopping experience for the customer more positive. Advances in technology have meant that Marks and Spencer have a website to sell their products. This makes it easier for customers to buy their products. The website also includes the whole range of products, which means customers can choose products that may not be available in their local Marks and Spencer store. The website also allows customers to track their orders, which means that customers can get information about when their order is likely to arrive, so they are less likely to miss deliveries, making the shopping experience more positive. The website also has a live chat option, which is a quick and easy way for customers to contact the business out of hours with any queries or complaints. The Marks and Spencer Facebook® page is another way of quickly dealing with queries and complaints, as well as being a way for the company to let their customers know about, e.g. any offers, changes to store opening times etc.

Section 4 — Human Resources

Page 46 — Recruitment

Q1 a) A process where a business thinks in depth about every little detail of a job.

b) Any two from: e.g. it is cheaper. / The post can be filled more quickly. / The new recruit will already know a lot about the firm. / The bosses may already know the candidate well.

Page 49 — Financial Motivation

Q1 It might increase their productivity, as the cleaners will feel more motivated to work for the hotel. They will want the hotel to be successful, so they will do their jobs well to help this happen.

Page 51 — Case Study — Human Resources

Q1 E.g. it's much cheaper to advertise on noticeboards than it is to advertise in the local or national press.

Q2 E.g. it may not be worth paying for full-time staff as the cafe is only likely to get busy during certain periods.

Q3 Any two from: e.g. they will get paid for the work they do. / They get 30% off food at any Lekker Lunch cafe. / There is a possibility of promotion within the company.

Q4 E.g. an advantage is that less communication is needed within the business, so changes can be made more quickly / the supervisor may be more motivated to work as they may feel more valued in the business. A disadvantage is that inconsistencies may develop between the different branches as each supervisor will make different decisions.

Q5 Hint: You need to discuss the advantages of induction training and the disadvantages of on-the-job training.
E.g. Induction training may have meant that the new staff were properly introduced to other workers and made to feel welcome in the business. This may have made them feel more valued and less likely to want to leave so quickly. During induction training the new staff may have been given some structured training on how to do their job before they started working in the cafe. This may have meant that they were less likely to make mistakes and felt more confident when they started their job. During the on-the-job training the supervisor may have passed on some of their bad habits to the new staff, meaning that they didn't

feel confident that they were doing their job properly. It may also have been difficult for the supervisor to give on-the-job training to all ten new staff members, meaning that staff weren't trained properly and they continued to make mistakes.

Section 5 — Marketing

Page 56 — Using Market Research

Q1 a) quantitative
b) qualitative

Page 61 — More on Product Development

Q1 Hint — you should describe a range of factors that will affect how well the product will sell, including the brand image and the design mix.
E.g. the business should consider what the market's needs are and whether those needs are being met already by competitors. It should also consider the brand image of the product and whether it will be strong enough to compete in the new market. The new product should also fulfil its function as an appropriate source of food for cats, the cost should be appropriate, and the packaging should be attractive to customers.

Page 63 — Pricing Strategies

Q1 E.g. the supermarket is using a loss leader pricing strategy. It might be using this strategy so that customers come into the store to buy a steak pie and then also buy other, profitable products while they are there.

Page 68 — More on E-Commerce

Q1 a) E.g. GAST won't have all of the costs associated with owning a high street store. This means they can afford to sell goods for less and still make a profit.

b) E.g. some customers might like the experience of visiting a physical jewellery shop to see the goods and try things on while they are choosing what to buy.

c) E.g. they may need to buy and install specialist equipment and train staff on how to use it. They may also need to pay a specialist website designer to update their website.

Page 69 — Case Study — Marketing

Q1 Any two from: e.g. consumers are only likely to want to purchase small quantities of cereals at a time, so it would be expensive for Nestlé® to have to distribute all of the orders directly to customers. / Selling to wholesalers and retailers means that products are available from more sources, meaning more consumers are able to buy them. / Selling to wholesalers means that Nestlé® will get bulk orders so they don't have to store lots of stock. / Retailers would be able to help promote Nestlé® products. / Retailers can provide customer service, which can help to increase sales.

Q2 Hint: Talk about the pros and cons of producing television adverts and how appropriate this method was for Nestlé®. Use information from the case study to analyse the success of the advert and explain how this success is likely to have affected sales.
E.g. although television adverts are expensive, they are seen by a wide audience and can deliver long messages. This method of advertising was appropriate for Nestle® as they are a big company that can afford the advertising costs. Breakfast cereals are eaten by many different types of people across the country, so using TV adverts is a good way for Nestlé® to target a wide audience. The adverts were very popular and Nestlé® went on to develop a successful Facebook® page using the Knitting Nana characters. The Facebook® page will have continued to promote the brand, with over 250 000 people being fans of the site. The Knitting Nanas are likely to have created lots of positive awareness of the brand, meaning that people would be more tempted to buy it, so sales are likely to have increased.

Q3 Shreddies Max would have been called a question mark when it was launched. This is because it was a new product so would have had a low market share, but it would have had high market growth because, e.g. consumers

were buying more and more cereals with a higher protein content.

Q4 Hint: Make sure you back up whatever two reasons you choose with information from the case study.
E.g. with cereal sales falling and customers being concerned about high levels of sugar in some cereals, some of the more sugary cereals made by Nestlé® might be in decline. Having a new product will help to balance the portfolio. Another reason Nestlé® might have chosen to launch Shreddies Max is to meet the needs of the target market, as consumers are opting for foods with a higher protein content.

Q5 Hint: In your answer make sure you consider the benefits of Nestlé® making their decision based on market research, as well as the limitations of the type of market research the decision is based upon.
E.g. putting the price on the packaging should help to increase sales as market research found that 82% of people shopping in a convenience store would specifically seek out products with the price on the packaging. However, the decision was made based on secondary research, which was only about shoppers in convenience stores and was not specifically about breakfast cereals. It would have cost Nestlé® money to change the packaging and it might not have had the impact on sales they were hoping for, meaning it might not have been as profitable as they expected.

Section 6 — Finance

Page 73 — Investments

Q1 Overall profit = 26 − 14 = 12m
Average annual profit = 12m ÷ 3 years = 4m
ARR = (average annual profit ÷ initial investment) × 100
= (4 ÷ 14) × 100 = **28.6%** (1 d.p.)

Page 78 — Cash Flow — Problems

Q1 Any two from: e.g. they could reduce customer credit. / They could reduce outflow/sell unsold products instead of making more. / They could arrange an overdraft with their bank. / They could arrange a new source of finance. / They could increase cash inflow/increase sales.

Page 81 — Profit Margins

Q1 Hint: cost of sales = opening stock + purchases − closing stock
cost of sales = 15 000 + 45 000 − 20 000
= 40 000
gross profit = revenue − cost of sales
= 200 000 − 40 000 = 160 000
gross profit margin = (gross profit ÷ revenue) × 100
= (160 000 ÷ 200 000) × 100
= 0.8 × 100 = **80%**

Page 83 — More on Statements of Financial Position

Q1 a) £4m + £6m = **£10m**

b) Retained profit is the profit that a firm decides to keep instead of paying in dividends.

Page 86 — Case Study — Finance

Q1 retained profit = net profit − taxation − dividends
= 17 467 − 1580 − 2300 = **£13 587**

Q2 Net profit margin = net profit ÷ revenue × 100
(17 467 ÷ 129 000) = 0.1354...
0.1354... × 100 = **13.5%** (3 s.f.)

Q3 113 000 − 129 000 = −16 000
−16 000 ÷ 129 000 = −0.1240... × 100
= **−12.4%**, or a **12.4% decrease** (3 s.f.)

Q4 Hint: To find out why the company made a loss from the income statement, look at what values have changed dramatically from one year to the next.
E.g. the company purchased too much stock throughout the year / the cost of sales was much higher than for the previous year.

Q5 E.g. it could compare its own finances with those of a competitor. It could compare statements of financial position from consecutive years.

Answers

Glossary

advertising	Any message that a firm pays for, which promotes the firm or its products.
ARR	The average rate of return on an investment.
asset	A valuable item owned by a business, or money owed to the business.
average unit cost	How much each product costs to make (calculated by dividing total costs by output).
Boston Matrix	A method used to analyse a business's product portfolio. Products are plotted according to their market share and how fast the market they are in is growing.
break-even output	The level of output at which a company's total revenue equals its total costs.
business plan	An outline of what a business will do and how it aims to do it.
capital	A company's wealth in the form of money or other assets.
capital employed	The total amount of money put into a business.
cash flow	The flow of all money into and out of a business.
cash inflow	Money that flows into a business.
cash outflow	Money that flows out of a business.
centralised organisation	An organisation with a structure in which all major decisions are made by one person or a few senior managers at the top of the hierarchy.
chain of command	The chain connecting directors to operatives in an organisational hierarchy.
channel of distribution	The way that products get from a manufacturer to a consumer.
commission	Money paid to sales staff for every item they sell on top of their basic salary.
competitive pricing	A pricing strategy in which a firm charges similar prices to other firms.
competitor	A business that sells the same products in the same market as another business.
consumer	The person who uses a good or service.
contract of employment	A legal agreement between an employee and their employer about a job.
cost	An expense paid out to run a business.
cost-plus pricing	A pricing strategy in which the cost of making the product is increased by a certain percentage to work out the price the product will be sold for.
credit	An agreement that a customer will pay for something at a later date.
credit terms	The terms of a credit agreement that tell a customer how long they have to pay.
current asset	An asset that doesn't last very long (e.g. cash).
current liability	A debt that a business has to pay off soon.
customer service	Any interaction a business has with its customers.
decentralised organisation	An organisation with a structure in which the authority to make most decisions is shared between people at different layers of the hierarchy.
delayering	Removing layers of management from an organisation.

delegation	Passing tasks or responsibilities onto another person.
demand	How much of a product people will be willing to buy at a given price.
depreciation	The amount of value that assets have lost over time due to wear and tear.
design mix	The different elements of design needed to make a product successful, including its function, cost and appearance.
diseconomy of scale	When growth leads to an increase in average unit cost.
dividend	A payment that a shareholder gets if the company makes a profit.
e-commerce	Buying and selling products on the internet.
economy of scale	A reduction in average unit cost that comes from producing on a large scale.
enterprise	The process of identifying new business opportunities, and then taking advantage of them.
entrepreneur	Someone who takes on the risks of enterprise activity.
exchange rate	A value that tells you how much one unit of a currency costs in a different currency.
extension strategy	An action intended to extend the life of a product.
external expansion	When a company grows by working with other businesses.
external recruitment	Where a business recruits new people from outside the business.
factor of production	A limited resource used to provide a good or service — e.g. land, labour, capital or enterprise.
fixed asset	An asset that a business keeps long-term or uses repeatedly — e.g. property, equipment, land, computers.
fixed cost	A cost that doesn't vary with output.
flat hierarchy	An organisational hierarchy with few layers.
flow production	A method of production in which all products are identical and are made as quickly as possible.
franchise	Where a company lets another firm sell its products or use its trademarks in return for a fee or a percentage of the profits.
fringe benefit	Any reward for an employee that is not part of their regular income.
full-time staff	Employees that generally work 35-40 hours a week.
globalisation	The process by which the world is becoming more interconnected.
government grant	A sum of money which is given by the government and does not have to be repaid.
gross profit	The profit left over once the cost of sales has been taken away from the total revenue.
gross profit margin	The fraction of every pound spent by customers that doesn't go towards making the product.
hire purchase	When a firm purchases something by first paying a deposit and then paying the rest in installments over a period of time, while they have use of the product.
income statement	A financial statement that shows how the income of a business has changed over a time period.
incorporated	A business that has its own legal identity.
induction training	A training program that introduces new employees to a workplace.

interest rate	A value which shows the cost of borrowing money or the reward given for saving money.
internal expansion	When a company grows by expanding its own activities (also called organic growth).
internal recruitment	Where existing employees are recruited into new roles within a business.
investment	Money which is put into a business to make improvements in order to make the business more profitable.
job analysis	A process in which every little detail of a job is thought about.
job description	A written description of what a job involves.
job production	A method of production in which each product has a unique design based on the customer's specification.
job share	Where the work and pay of one full-time job is shared between two people.
just-in-case (JIC)	A method used in stock management in which buffer stocks of items are kept at every stage of the production process.
just-in-time (JIT)	A method used in production or stock management in which stock levels are kept at a bare minimum — products are made just in time for delivery to customers.
lean production	A production strategy that aims to use as few resources as possible and to have as little waste as possible.
limited liability	Where the owners of a business are not legally responsible for all the debts a business has.
liquidity	How easily an asset can be converted into money.
loan	A long-term source of money that must be paid back to the lender.
logistics	Getting goods or services from one part of the supply chain to another.
long-term liability	A debt that a business has to pay off over a long period of time.
loss	Where the total costs for a company over a period of time are greater than its revenue.
loss leader pricing	A pricing strategy in which the price of a product is set below cost.
m-commerce	When goods and services are bought on the internet using a wireless mobile device, such as a smartphone or tablet.
margin of safety	The gap between current level of output and the break-even output.
market	A meeting place between customers and suppliers, trade in a particular type of product or the potential customers for a product.
market research	When a business investigates different aspects of a market, e.g. demand for a product, the competition and the target market.
market share	The proportion of total sales within a market that is controlled by a business.
market size	The number of individuals (including companies) within a market that are potential buyers and sellers of products, or the total value of products in the market.
marketing mix	The four elements that must be considered for good marketing: product, price, promotion and place.
merger	When two companies join together to form a new, larger firm.
mortgage	A loan used to finance buying property.
net profit margin	The fraction of every pound spent by customers that the company gets to keep.

Glossary

off-the-job training	A method of training in which an employee learns <u>away</u> from their workplace.
on-the-job training	A method of training in which an employee is <u>shown</u> how to do their job by <u>another employee</u> and then given the opportunity to <u>practise</u>.
operating profit	The money left over after paying <u>all the costs</u> of running the business.
opportunity cost	The value of something that's <u>given up</u> in order to do something else.
organic growth	When a company grows by <u>expanding its own activities</u> (also called internal expansion).
outsourcing	When a business pays <u>another firm</u> to carry out tasks it could do <u>itself</u>.
overdraft	When <u>more money</u> is taken <u>out</u> of a bank account than has been <u>paid into</u> it.
part-time staff	Employees that generally work <u>10-30 hours</u> a week.
partnership	A business ownership structure in which a small number of people (usually between 2 and 20) own an <u>unincorporated company</u>.
person specification	A list of the <u>qualifications</u>, <u>experience</u>, <u>skills</u> and <u>attitudes</u> a person needs for a particular job.
price penetration	A <u>pricing strategy</u> in which a firm charges a <u>very low price</u> for a product when it is <u>new</u>.
price skimming	A <u>pricing strategy</u> in which a firm charges a <u>high price</u> for a product <u>to begin with</u>.
primary research	<u>Market research</u> that involves getting information from <u>customers</u> or <u>potential</u> customers.
private limited company	A business ownership structure that is <u>incorporated</u> and has shares, but the shares can only be sold with the agreement of <u>all the shareholders</u>.
procurement	The act of <u>finding</u> and <u>buying</u> things that a business needs from <u>outside</u> of the business.
product life cycle	The different <u>stages</u> that a product goes through <u>over time</u>.
product portfolio	The <u>range</u> of different products that a business sells.
profit	The difference between <u>revenue</u> and <u>costs</u> over a period of time.
promotional mix	The <u>combination</u> of different <u>promotional methods</u> a firm uses to promote a product.
public limited company	A business ownership structure that is <u>incorporated</u> and has shares that can be bought and sold by <u>anyone</u>.
public relations (PR)	Business activities which involve communicating with the <u>media</u> in an attempt to <u>promote</u> a firm or its products to the <u>public</u>.
purchasing economy of scale	A reduction in <u>average unit cost</u> that comes from a firm being offered a <u>lower unit cost</u> from suppliers when it buys its supplies <u>in bulk</u>.
qualitative information	Information that involves people's <u>feelings</u> or <u>opinions</u>.
quantitative information	Information that can be <u>measured</u> or reduced to a <u>number</u>.
retailer	A business that <u>sells</u> products to <u>consumers</u>.
retained profit	Profit that is <u>put back</u> into the business.
revenue	The <u>income</u> earned by a business in a given <u>time period</u>.
salary	A <u>fixed payment</u> that is made to employees <u>every month</u>.
sales process	A series of steps for <u>finding</u> and <u>selling to</u> customers, as well as providing <u>customer service</u>.

sales promotion	A short-term method used to boost a firm's sales, e.g. 2 for 1 offers.
secondary research	Market research that involves looking at data from outside the business, e.g. market reports.
segmentation	When people within a market are divided into different groups.
share	A unit of ownership in a company. Owners of shares can share in the profits of the company.
share capital	The money put into a business when shares were originally issued.
sole trader	A business ownership structure where one person owns an unincorporated company.
span of control	The number of workers who report to one manager in a hierarchy.
sponsorship	A method of promotion in which a business gives money to an organisation or event. In return the organisation or event displays the business's name.
staff retention	When a business keeps its staff.
stakeholder	Any individual or group of people that is affected by a business.
start-up capital	The money or assets needed to set up a business.
statement of financial position	A financial statement that records a business's assets and liabilities at a particular moment in time.
supply chain	The group of firms that are involved in all the various processes required to make a finished product or service available to the customer.
sustainability	Working in a way that doesn't damage the Earth for future generations.
takeover	When an existing business expands by buying more than half the shares in another firm.
tall hierarchy	An organisational hierarchy with lots of layers.
technical economy of scale	A reduction in average unit cost that comes from a firm being able to afford more advanced machinery or use larger premises than a smaller firm.
telesales	Selling products to consumers via phone.
total quality management (TQM)	A strategy that aims to make quality the responsibility of every employee in an organisation.
trade credit	When businesses give firms time to pay for certain purchases.
unincorporated	A business that doesn't have its own legal identity.
unlimited liability	Where the owners of a business are legally responsible for all the debts a business has.
USP (unique selling point)	This is some feature that makes a product different from its competitors.
variable cost	A cost that increases as a firm expands output.
wage	Payment that is usually made to employees weekly or monthly. It is calculated using a time rate or a piece rate.
wholesaler	A business that buys products in bulk and stores them in a warehouse.
working capital	The money available for the day-to-day operating of the business.
zero hours contract	A contract of employment which means the employer doesn't have to offer the employee any work at all and the employee doesn't have to accept any work that is offered to them.

Index

2 for 1 offers 65

A

advertising 58, 64
aims (of a business) 8
air pollution 23
application forms 47
appropriation account 79
apps 21, 39
assets 71, 72, 82-84
average rate of return (ARR) 73
average unit costs 11, 14

B

bank loans 25, 71, 72
billboards 64
Boston Matrix (Box) 59
brand image 61
break-even analysis 74, 75
business
    aims 8
    expansion 14-16
    location 13
    objectives 8-10
    opportunities 2
    plans 12, 29

C

capital 4
capital employed 83
cash 76, 82
cash flow 71, 76-78
centralisation 43
chain of command 42
channels of distribution 66
command words 89
commission 49
competition (in markets) 26
competitions 65
competitive pricing 63
consumer law 20
contracts of employment 45
cost-plus pricing 63
costs 11, 74
coupons 65
credit 71, 77, 78
creditors 78, 82
curriculum vitae (CVs) 47
customer service 36, 38, 39

D

debtors 82
decentralisation 43
delayering 43
delegation 42, 43
demand 54, 57
digital communication 21
discrimination 19
diseconomies of scale 14
diversification 60
dividends 10

E

e-commerce 15, 21, 39, 67, 68
economies of scale 14
employment law 19
enterprise 3, 4
entrepreneurs 3, 29
environmental issues (of a business) 23
Equality Act 2010 19
ethical issues (of a business) 8, 22
exam skills 88, 89
exchange rates 28
exports 28
extension strategies 58
external expansion (of a business) 16

F

factors of production 4
Fair Trade 22
finance (sources of) 71, 72
financial motivation 49
financial statements 79, 80, 82-85
    analysis of 80, 84, 85
fixed assets 72, 84
fixed costs 11, 74
flat organisational structures 42
flow production 34
focus groups 55
forecasts (cash flow) 76, 77
franchising 15, 37
free gifts 65
free samples 65
fringe benefits 50
full-time employment 45

G

gaps in the market 3, 26
globalisation 27
global warming 23
goods 2
government grants 71, 72
gross profit 79, 80
    margins 81, 85

H

Health and Safety at Work Act (1974) 19
hierarchies 42, 43
hire purchases 71, 72

I

ICT 21
imports 28
income 24
income statements 79, 80, 85, 86
    analysis of 80, 85
incorporated companies 6
induction training 48
interest rates 25
internal expansion (of a business) 15
internet
    advertising 64
    market research 55
interviews
    market research 55
    recruitment 47
investments 73, 80

J

job
    analysis 46
    descriptions 46
    roles (in a business) 42
    sharing 45
job production 34
just-in-case (JIC) 35
just-in-time (JIT) 35

L

lean production 35
legal structures (of a business) 5-7
liabilities (of a business) 82-84
limited companies 6-8, 10
limited liability 6, 7
liquidity 82
loans 71, 72
location (of a business) 13
logistics 33
loss 11, 74
loss leader pricing 63

M

management styles 50
margin of safety 75
market 26
>> opportunities 55
>> research 54-56, 61
>> segmentation 54
>> share 8, 54
>> size 54
marketing mix 53
m-commerce 67, 68
mergers 16
mortgages 71, 72
motivation of staff
>> financial 49
>> non-financial 50

N

National Living Wage 19
National Minimum Wage 19
net cash flow 76
net profit 79
>> margins 81, 85
noise pollution 23
non-financial motivation 50
not-for-profit organisations 7

O

objectives (of a business) 8-10
off-the-job training 48
on-the-job training 48
operating profits 79, 80
opportunity costs 4
organic growth (of a business) 15
organisational structures 42-44
outsourcing 15
overdrafts 71, 72
overtrading 78

P

part-time employment 45
partnerships 5
person specifications 46
place (marketing mix) 53, 66
point of sale displays 65
post sales service 38
price 53, 62, 63
>> penetration 63
>> skimming 63
pricing strategies 63
primary market research 55

primary sector 2
private limited companies (ltd) 6
procurement 33
product 53
>> development 60, 61
>> differentiation 61
>> life cycles 57
>> portfolios 59, 60
>> recalls 36
production efficiency 35
production methods 34
profit 11, 74
profit and loss account 79
profit sharing schemes 49
promotion (marketing mix) 53, 64, 65
promotional mix 65
public limited companies (plc) 6
public relations (PR) 65
purchasing economies of scale 14

Q

qualitative data 56
quality 36, 37
quantitative data 56
questionnaires 55

R

raw materials 2, 13
recruitment 46, 47
recycling 23
retailers 66
retained profits 72, 79, 80, 83, 84
return 73
revenue 11, 74, 79, 81
risks in business 29

S

salaries 49
sales process 38
sales promotions 65
secondary market research 55
secondary sector 2
segmentation (of a market) 54
selection process 47
services 2
share
>> capital 83
>> issues 72
shareholder value 8
shareholders 6, 10, 84
social media 21, 65
sole traders 5

span of control 42
spending (consumer) 25
sponsorship 64
staff retention 46
stakeholders 10, 84
start-up capital 71
starting a business 2
statements of financial position 82-85
>> analysis of 84, 85
stock 35, 79, 82
suppliers 10, 32, 33
supply chains 32, 33
surveys 55
sustainability 23

T

takeovers 16
tall organisational structures 42
target market 54
technical economies of scale 14
telesales 66
tertiary sector 2
total costs 11, 74
Total Quality Management (TQM) 37
trade credit 71
trade descriptions 20
trading account 79, 81
traffic congestion 23
training 48

U

uncertainties in business 29
unemployment 24
unique selling point (USP) 61
unlimited liability 5, 7

V

variable costs 11, 74

W

wages 49
waste 23
websites 21, 39
wholesalers 66
working capital 78, 82

Z

zero hour contracts 45